Primary First

First published in Great Britain in 2006 by
Primary First
57 Britannia Way
Lichfield
Staffordshire
WS14 9UY

Printed in the United Kingdom.

ISBN 0-9552526-0-1
ISBN 978-0-9552526-0-0

This book is dedicated to teachers all over the world who have held fast to the principles and practices of Creativity throughout their teaching.

"When distracted from the true purposes in our lives, we frequently find ourselves living in a lifestyle which does not seem of our own making. At that time, regrets are not enough; we must actively go back to first principles and our own beliefs, revisit them, cherish them and love them. Only then can we live in harmony with the world around us."

**(Roger Cole)**

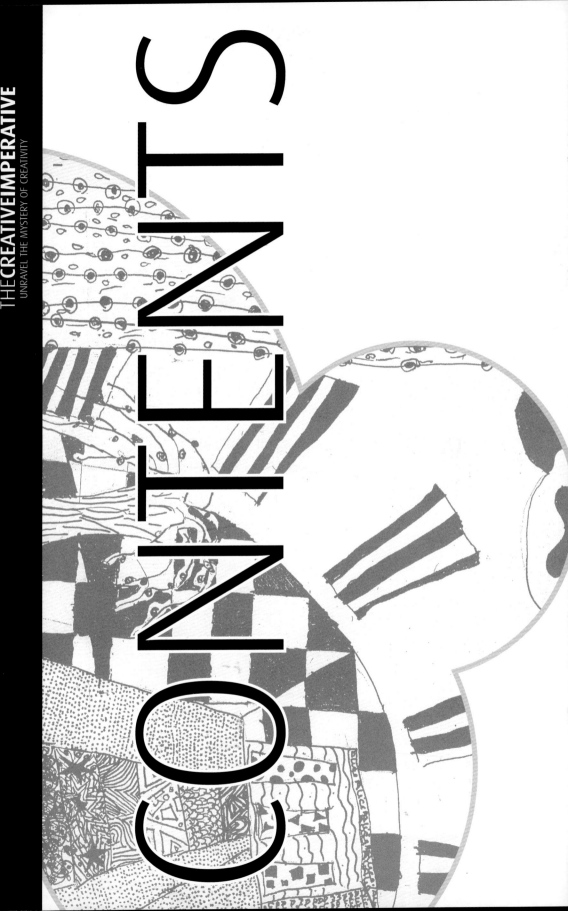

# CONTENTS

# CHAPTER 1: WHAT IS CREATIVITY?

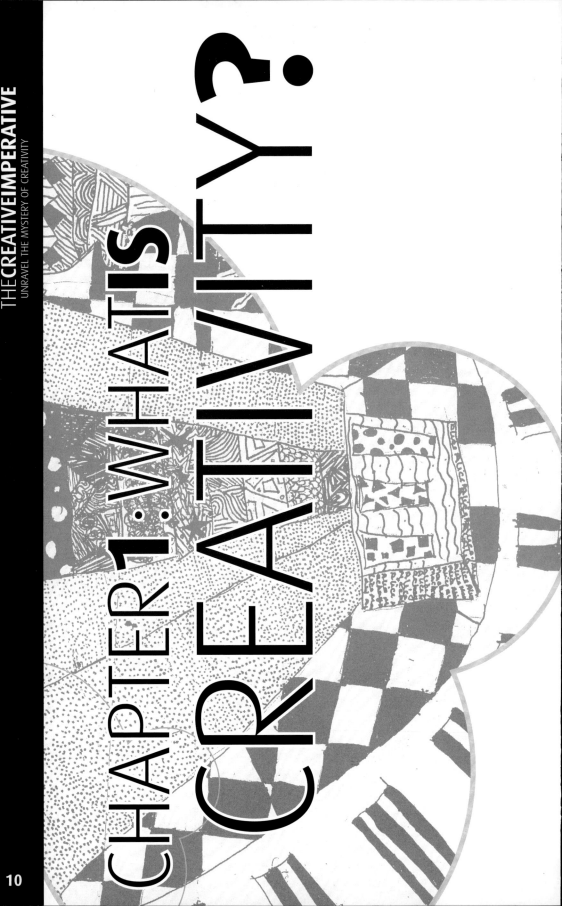

# CHAPTER**1**: **What Is Creativity?**

**A journalist once asked Pablo Picasso what creativity was.
Picasso replied, "I don't know and if I did I wouldn't tell you".**

It is no surprise, therefore, that so many misconceptions surround
the word 'creativity' in primary education. It has sometimes been
associated with learning behaviours which can only be described
as 'doing your own thing' or put more critically 'behaving in an
undisciplined way'. There are of course reasons for this confusion
of terminology, not least as there are numerous occasions when
adults, as well as children, are being creative, yet appear to be
aimlessly playing. It is however, far from true that this is either
the only or most important aspect of creativity. So, at the outset,
it seems only sensible to provide a number of definitions which
will go some way towards clarifying what creativity is, and is not,
and introduce phrases and terminologies which it embraces.

Creativity is not something which some people have and others
do not, although there are people of whom we say he or she
is a very creative person in contrast to someone who appears
not to be creative. Creativity is a function of intelligence and
can be found in any activity where human intelligence is actively
engaged. Since creativity is not solely a function of the arts, it
is likely that in every subject and aspect of the primary school
day there are opportunities for us to observe both teachers and
learners behaving creatively.

In its 1999 report All our Futures: Creativity Culture and Education, the National Advisory Committee on Creative and Cultural Education (NACCCE) defined creativity as:

Imaginative activity fashioned so as to produce outcomes that are both original and of value.

The report suggests that creative processes have four characteristics:

- First, they always involve thinking or behaving imaginatively

- Second, this imaginative activity is purposeful: that is, it is directed to achieve an objective

- Third, these processes must generate something original

- Fourth, the outcome must be of value in relation to the objective

These four characteristics will be revisited regularly in subsequent chapters and examples given.

To put it more simply, when the Year 2 teacher asked her pupils to define creativity, seven year old Jerome wrote, 'Creativity is when you make something out of something else that hasn't been invented yet'.

The two essential elements of creativity which are unique to human intelligence are the capacity to imagine and the power of symbolic and systematic thinking. We need to understand how imagination and systematic and symbolic thinking are different and what the consequences of these processes can be. Thinking is transformed when intelligence is stimulated to imagine, create and invent new symbols and new ideas. When these behaviours are combined and are observed by others it often leads to exclamations such as, "Now why didn't I think of that"?

*[handwritten marginal note: → can we assess creativity? analyse]*

It is also apparent that different people, scientists, mathematicians, writers, poets, dancers, designers, gymnasts and other professionals express their creativity in different ways. Anyone who develops their creativity does so through a medium – it is their 'means' of expression. Finding the medium may occur quite naturally but for some it is a lifelong task. Whilst some people find their medium at an early age others may not find it until later in life, if at all.

Creativity and age do not therefore follow any set chronological developmental pattern. One cannot say that the older you are or the more experienced you are, the more creative you will be. Many teachers will know of very young children who have shown outstanding creative abilities and who later in life have been unable to maintain or repeat their earlier skills and talents – they lose their creativity.

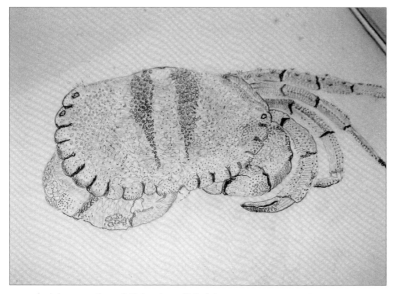

*How old was the child who did this? Is it Art or Science?*

In contrast there are others who have followed what appears to be a normal pattern of development who have become highly creative adults at later stages in their lives.

In the classroom, good teachers generally develop skills and routines in learning with their children and in time encourage them to adopt them as their own – the old adage 'practice makes perfect'. It goes without saying that the child who has a range of expressive skills, will find expressing themselves a relatively easy task. Consequently in order to develop creativity, teachers seek to provide skills which give children insights into the world around them. A key skill in learning to study that world is to learn how to look and this is best done from an early age through drawing.

"I don't know what I may seem to the world, but, as to myself, I seem to have been only like a boy playing on the sea shore and divesting myself, now and then finding a smoother pebble or a prettier shell than ordinary, whilst the great ocean of truth lay all undiscovered before me"

W Wordsworth

# Aimless & Purposeful

## "Doing your own thing"

Some people mistakenly imagine that unconventional behaviour is in itself creative, or that by merely doing something differently from others around you, is to be creative. This of course is misleading, since if this idea were developed, madness would be the most evident expression of creativity.

Dryden wrote "Great wits are sure to madness, near allied". It is that turn of mind, that behaviour, which compels an adult or a child to 'swim against the tide', to take an unusual standpoint, to diverge from the norm in order to look for something new which frequently distinguishes the adult or child as being creative. Of course, both adult and child in the extremes of that behaviour can cause concern to others as well. In adults it has caused men and women to be pilloried or ostracised, in children it can lead to reprimand or even expulsion from school. Extremes of behaviour are not readily accepted by a society that prefers everyone to conform to accepted principles.

Beethoven brought the symphonic form to a level of expressive power that had never been attempted by anyone before him, Picasso overthrew the conventions of representation in painting, Einstein challenged the orders of thinking in science in proposing the Theory of Relativity and Joyce introduced arresting structure to literary narrative. All challenged conventions but in doing so, played around with ideas and challenged accepted viewpoints.

It is little different in the Primary Classroom. I can distinctly remember as a young teacher, being told that we did real work in the morning, maths and writing, and creativity in the afternoon. The afternoons seemed to me at the time to be an opportunity for little or no structure, everyone, teachers and children 'doing their own thing'. Sometimes to be fair, with some teachers the product was exceptional and distinctive but with others it was a recipe for chaos!

This recollection provides something of an insight into why there has been such concern in the last twenty years about creativity in primary education. It has seemed that in the hands of some teachers who are said to be creative, success is evident. The outcome of interaction between teacher and child, between child and materials produces distinctive and original work, whilst the remainder – sometimes the majority – flounder; even drown in an unruly riot of free expression which can truly be described as disaster! It would be possible to describe numerous classrooms where chaos has obviously reigned under the misconceptions of creativity whilst in complete contrast the disciplining of apparent chaos can stifle the very exploration which feeds the imagination with the endless possibilities on which creativity thrives.

So 'doing your own thing' can be aimless or can be purposeful and it is one of those aspects of teaching and learning where enormous risks have to be taken by the teacher in order to know the boundaries of experimentation, exploration and free expression. There are times when exceptional teachers seem to 'preside over chaos', but the vigilant observer will soon notice that there are boundaries which these teachers exercise which are clearly understood in terms of behaviour, use of materials and respect for tools and equipment. When these teachers are seen at their best they are not unlike the conductor of an orchestra, who at a signal can expect total attention and silence from what moments earlier was a cacophony of unrelated sounds as musicians 'warmed' to the task of 'tuning up'.

Inevitably, the notion of creativity presents problems, for without doubt the teachers' task is simplified by all the children sitting down, all facing the same way, the distance between each child being far enough for there to be no possibility of bodily contact, and of course silence. Whilst there are occasions when this arrangement for learning is desirable, there are many occasions when it is not. For example, when a teacher wants a class of children to generate ideas by discussion in small groups to develop their own thinking, this kind of rigid framework can inhibit the kind of learning the teacher seeks to promote.

It is very difficult for the teacher to let go, for the control to come from within the child, rather than being externally imposed by the teacher. So there is a balance which is essential between total freedom and total dominance, between inhibition and spontaneity. The outstanding teacher 'manages' chaos and what appears to be spontaneous is frequently meticulously planned and prepared for. Understanding the term 'doing your own thing' has a critical part to play in coming to terms with the difficulties of enabling creativity to thrive:

> **Too much freedom – chaos can ensue.**
> **Too much control – creativity can be stifled.**

# Some Have It Some Do Not

## "Geniuses aren't born, they're created"

Oscar Wilde

Throughout our history men and women like Beethoven and Lisa Meitner (whose extension of Einstein's thinking led her to split the atom) have changed the course of our lives and reshaped the world through their visionary ideas. Every generation must wonder whether in their lives there could be anyone as visionary and creative as those who preceded them. Leonardo de Vinci's visionary and creative ideas have largely not been superseded by the generations who have followed him, but they have been developed and built upon. Man's first powered flight came hundreds of years after Leonardo's first ideas. As a child Mozart had extraordinary gifts in musical composition whilst other children born in the same year had none. From examples like this we have concluded that some children are born with exceptional creative talent whilst others are not. But whilst Mozart was highly creative at a very early age, it did not exclude others from being creative and developing creative skills at a later stage of their development. Creativity is not a special quality confined to certain people as a birthright; it can be nurtured, taught and developed if it is clearly understood.

# It Gets Better With Age

## "I have always wanted to paint with the eyes of a child"

Picasso

Young children know few boundaries and as a consequence they frequently bring together disparate ideas as they juggle with new and exciting experiences.  They know little of defined boundaries and behave intuitively, sometimes with startling results. Unfortunately there has been evidence throughout the history of education, of a gradual decline in creativity in young children largely, I believe, as a result of a realization that conformity to specific rules is a prerequisite of satisfactory achievement.  This no doubt led to Peter Ustinov's headmaster writing in his report 'This boy has exceptional individuality which must be suppressed at all costs'.

Systematic symbols and their uses are advocated as being of greater value and importance than schematic symbols.  This was exemplified by the 2003 National Literacy Writing Task at Key Stage Two.  Having spent six years building a rich vocabulary, learning how to use adjectives and adverbs to enrich text, inverted commas to identify speech and the myriad of other skills within the National Literacy Framework; the day eventually came to demonstrate the culmination of all that effort and study in "the test".

## The subject, "The Queue"

Is there anyone who could be  inspired as a writer, in response to four pictures of a Queue? In a world so lacking in imagination, this indeed was a victory for systematic measures and a desperately sad day for children and the proposition of educational potential.

So how many frustrated creative children were left behind at the starting gate of this exercise. It can be of little surprise that teachers who aspire to higher orders of teaching and learning despair when their aspirations are dumbed-down by such abysmal levels of conformity.

Throughout our history there have equally been men and women described as frustrated, creative geniuses. Sometimes the turmoil of creativity in their lives spills over to such an extent that it destroys the person entirely. In contrast we know of many men and women whose visionary ideas and imagination caused them to redefine the boundaries of science, music, art or commerce; they in fact, in their own way, reshaped the world.

So there is a rich potential for creativity at every age and every stage and it is clear that those adults who come to find their creative talents late or later in life will do so as a result of circumstances, often beyond their control, whilst others may strive to find a meaningful, creative role in their lives with limited or little success. I believe that every child can be taught to develop their creative potential. It therefore follows that teachers need to be clear about what creativity is in order to develop it. When we refer to children or adults being creative, they are generally doing something. Creativity is not a passive behaviour; on the contrary it actively shapes something such as words, movements, sounds or materials. The action or series of actions changes what it acts on or is in conjunction with, and in some ways reshapes or redefines it, sometimes for ever.

In the classroom, children can be creative in, for example, their writing, their science, music or mathematics – they cannot be creative in the abstract. When creative activity takes place there is always a consequence of the action. With different children at different stages of development, this kind of action is likely to be circumscribed by the opportunities for experience and the development of skills.

# The Essential Elements Imagination

## "What is now proved was once only imagined"

William Blake

In the Introduction I described the two essential elements of creativity which are unique to human intelligence, as the capacity to imagine and the power of symbolic and systematic thinking. Let us now consider their importance in greater depth.

Imagination is an important dimension of creativity. To use one's imagination is sometimes regarded as a prerequisite of creative thinking but can also be referred to in a critical or derogatory way. I can recall a teacher in school sarcastically saying to a child, "The trouble with you is that you have too vivid an imagination". I remember wondering at the time, what the trouble was with that. Reflecting on the circumstances I suppose the teacher was not getting the kind of conditional response from the child which she wanted. In fact, the response was everything but conditional and was probably far too removed from the teacher's expectation of the kind of response that she felt was appropriate.

In a different context I can also remember demanding of a child that they use their imagination in order to improve the quality of a piece of work. At the time I did not consider what it was that I wanted to happen, or how or why. In fact, it was a dismissive direction. "Go and use your imagination"; as if the child could go and plug in to some think tank which would change their work for the better.

My third recollection is hearing a teacher actively encouraging children to be imaginative in order to help them to enrich or develop an idea. In this instance the intonation of the voice changed to one of enticement and encouragement. "Now let's try and imagine what it would be like if ........". The phrasing of the invitation anticipated that there didn't seem to be a right or wrong answer, the opportunity was open-ended and it seemed that many different responses could be accepted, varying in degrees of imagination.

"A popular cliché in philosophy says that Science is pure analysis, like taking a rainbow to pieces and that Art is pure synthesis, putting the rainbow together. This is not so. All imagination begins by analysing nature"

A Einstein

The imagination is a uniquely distinguishing feature of the human mind. We can only assume it is not present in other animals and therefore is unique to human beings. The imagination helps us to generate new ideas that were not previously in existence. We have become so accustomed to this unique human quality that we have phrases like 'in the minds eye' to describe how we are imagining. This means that we generate an image in our minds which can be from the past, present or anticipating the future. It can even be a composite of all three since there are no boundaries of right or wrong in the imagination. From the past we can recall a place and time and imagine what it would have been like if the circumstances had been different.

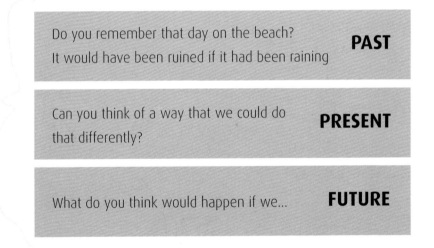

Do you remember that day on the beach?
It would have been ruined if it had been raining          **PAST**

Can you think of a way that we could do
that differently?          **PRESENT**

What do you think would happen if we...          **FUTURE**

Through our imagination we also have the ability to mix real and invented images to this kind of thinking, some which may not even exist – composites of people, animals or birds, places and events, feelings or experiences.

"Do you remember that day on the beach when that huge, blue and green monster emerged from the sea and chased everyone off the beach?"

"Can you imagine what it would be like if we fixed wings to that elephant which were big enough so that it could fly to the moon?"

"What would it be like if cats and dogs were twice the size of human beings and they looked after us instead of us looking after them?"

In these examples your imagination is being called upon to generate images of which you have little or no experience or to develop ideas beyond experience. These are images which are hypothetical, composed in your mind and only exist there. They are unique to you, you can share your explanations of them with others but no one can imagine the way you imagine, no-one can imagine for you. In this way each individual's imagination is unique to them.

In the classroom children show us how well their imagination is developed by the images they use. A class of children in Key Stage 1 were encouraged to develop large drawings of dragons over an extended period of time. Once they had decided on the overall shape of their dragon they began to work on the detail. The monsters became images created from all the knowledge and understanding the children had of birds, insects, humans and animals rearranged in their own unique way. No one drawing was the same as another since each showed the active knowledge each child had of the world around them – their schemata. So different horns, eyes, toes, tails, feet, scales were developed in different ways, based on previous experience and the capacity to invent, extemporise or pretend.

One distinct difference between imagination and creativity is particularly important. I have already suggested that you cannot be passively creative – you are creative with something and change occurs as consequence of that action. Imagination is exactly the opposite to this and can be totally passive – it is a private and personal happening which no one need even know is taking place. You can be with someone else and they can have no idea of your imaginings! You may of course give clues to your private thoughts, such as a wry smile, and be asked what you are thinking about. You can deny any thought, "Oh, it's nothing", or you can offer your imagining, "I was just imagining what it would be like if....".

So imagination, which plays such a vital part in childhood, has behaviours in school which teachers actively encourage as a way of helping children to extend and develop their experience, such that it comes from within them. Of equal importance, it stays with them in varying degrees throughout their life. "The willing suspension of disbelief ....." is an important, well known characteristic of role play. Whilst it is a ready behaviour of adults watching for example, live theatre or a television drama, for children it can be a daily behaviour arising from any aspect of the curriculum. But, just as adults share or hold onto their private and personal imaginings so in school, children are frequently encouraged to engage in both kinds of activities and to share and often record their imaginings in different ways through a variety of different materials. The place of dressing-up and playing out a role is frequently undervalued in primary schools and yet its value for many children is of measurable importance.

The child, and the adult for that matter, chooses a way of interpreting their imagining and it is through this application that imagining is manifested in creativity. Creativity is, in fact, the application of imagination – the application involves taking action to produce something and as a consequence of that, a change takes place.

*Curriculum innovation and planning. Children reliving experiences in order to better understand.*

"Discovery is not strictly a logical performance and accordingly we may describe the obstacle to be overcome in solving a problem as a logical gap and speak of the width of the gap as the measure of ingenuity required for solving the problem. Imagination is the leap by which the logical gap is crossed, the plunge by which we gain a foothold on another shore of reality. On such plunges the artist or scientist has to stake bit by bit, his entire professional life".

If we apply these principles to a child imagining a dragon, the availability of clay provides the child with the chance of translating their thinking into a three dimensional material; so the child shapes the material to interpret the idea and as I shall discuss later, the appropriateness of the material assists or limits the expression of the idea.

In the classroom, other opportunities could occur to interpret the dragon, for example in dance. The only difference from the point of view of outcome is that when the activity is completed, clay provides concrete evidence of the activity of the interpretation, whereas the dance exists in its own right and although there has been an active interpretive process taking place, nothing remains when it is complete unless it has been recorded on video. This of course does not make it any the less valid.

# Symbolic And Systematic Thinking

## "We need children who think with real conviction"

Christian Schiller

In order to understand the importance of symbolic and systematic thought it may help to consider what kind of thinking human beings do which distinguishes them from other animals. Humans are unique in having the capacity for symbolic and systematic thought. **Systematic symbols** are of equal importance to **schematic symbols** but regrettably schematic symbols are regarded by many schools as being of secondary importance to systematic ones.

## Systematic symbols

Systematic symbols are prescribed by rules and accepted codes of practice to express precise meaning. The arrangements of the symbols are largely predetermined so as to make sense and a whole range of encoding procedures is taught and learnt, in order that the systematic symbols and their precise meaning or meanings are clearly understood. There is little latitude for interpretation on an individual basis and the child gains the sense of the meaning through recognition of how the rules are applied and interpreted.

The most obvious example is the development of language in young children. I recently met a young boy and girl, twins, who because of their experiences as babies had noticeably underdeveloped language skills. They knew that sounds had meaning and had developed their own basic code of sounds, but depended on pointing or touching to communicate their needs, feelings and frustrations. Connecting sounds with meaning was for them in its most basic form. With new foster parents who talked with them continually, their language grew daily as their ability to connect sound with meaning grew. The ability of the young child, and later the adult, to connect sound with meaning is what makes all language possible. Words, appropriate words, help us to think about and share our experiences with others, but they do not help us to share all our experiences. Obviously words that are written down help us to share and record our experiences. So, quite obviously, schools have placed great emphasis on the ability of children to do this themselves and to be able to share the experiences of others through reading about other people's experiences which have been recorded in books.

It seems reasonable to ask therefore whether children and adults have thoughts that cannot be expressed through words alone, that their ideas need another means of expression? Words spoken or written have a linear structure, they start at the beginning if they are to make sense, are governed by the conventions of syntax and subsequently come to an end. Writing could be diagrammatically represented by a long chain, each link joined to the next, independent but interdependent on the links on either side.

## Schematic symbols

In contrast, some ideas are best assembled simultaneously in a picture. These ideas sometimes cannot find expression through words. The artist Turner's paintings of stormy seas have a descriptive totality which words cannot provide. The picture cannot be dissected into numerous tiny squares, or broken down into its component parts as we can break down a sentence or paragraph to better understand its meaning

*Snow Storm by Turner*

Turner's storm is an example of a schematic symbol. It is his unique interpretation and expression of a particular moment in his life and captures much of his own experience and feeling of that moment to which each of us can respond in our own way. The painting may evoke sadness, fear or a sense of wonder and no two people will have identical responses to it.

This makes appreciation difficult. Because there are no guaranteed responses, there can be no rules about how you should perceive or read the painting. There are no fixed and predetermined rules which provide the meaning for the symbolic forms of expression used in the painting. This applies equally of course to music, poetry and dance which also use schematic symbols to express their meaning. The viewer, observer or listener brings their own unique response to interpret the experience. So just as it does not help us at the outset to cut up Turner's Seascape into tiny squares to understand the whole picture, it is of little use at the outset to study one line of a score in an overture or a sequence of steps in a dance in order to understand or come to terms with

# Art, music and dance present our ideas in a schematic form.

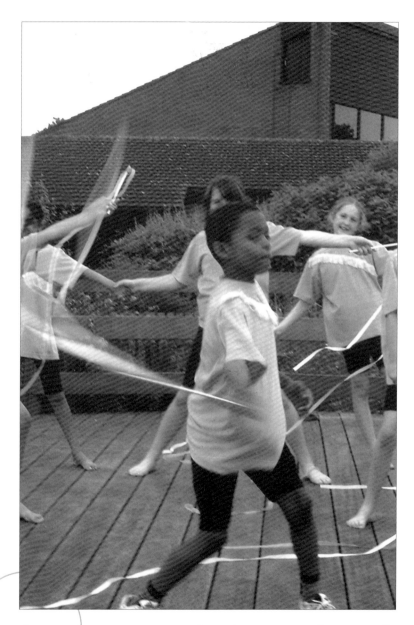

The two forms are not interdependent nor are they mutually exclusive of each other. Importantly, as far as this publication is concerned both systematic and schematic forms are major contributors to the creative process as means of expressing an idea.

# The Means Of Expression Finding The Medium

## "I can squirm just like a snake"

Boy aged 8

For many people, finding a suitable way to interpret their ideas is a lifelong task. If you have ideas and cannot find an appropriate means of expression for them, you are likely to become frustrated? So finding the medium is one of the keys to releasing creative potential.

'As the child shapes the material, so the material shapes the child'.

I recently watched a small boy attempting to make something out of plasticene. The material itself was hard, the room was cold and the heat from his hands did not soften the large, grubby lump to enable him to begin to shape it. He gave up, stood up and as he left the table, picked up a pencil and stabbed the lump several times. So much for a material suited to interpreting his ideas.

If creativity is a process – this suggests some sequence of events where a relationship is established between the creator and the medium. Whilst I am concerned in this book with the needs of the child, the arguments are just as relevant to the adult. Many of us will have tried to perform a task which in the hands of an expert looks so easy and yet when we attempt it, it is too difficult and we feel a sense of failure.

Watch the potter at his wheel, the clay rises and falls and changes shape seemingly at will. The wheel rotates at speed and every aspect of the success of the task depends on the speed of the wheel and its centrifugal forces, the potter's hands interpreting the form in his head. But of equal importance is the consistency of the clay – the medium. If the clay is too hard and not properly prepared, no potter, however great his skill, will ever make a pot. To succeed, the clay must first be centred and if it is too hard to ply itself to the potter's hand, he may as well not begin. To know the consistency of the clay, there has to be much time spent understanding its differing consistencies - too hard, too soft, too many air bubbles, too coarse.

To gain the knowledge which determines what you can do with it, the trainee potter needs to play, to have the freedom to experiment and take risks. In this way we get to "know our material". Ideally it is best to have this apprenticeship alongside a master potter, who knows that only through handling different kinds of clay can one know when the clay is ready to be worked.

When I went to Antibes to work in the Picasso pottery as a young student, I imagined I would be constructing fine vases. I was dismayed on the first day and in subsequent weeks, to spend the larger part of every day emptying the slurry bins and digging green clay from a pit to weather in the preparation troughs. Only years later did I realise how much I knew about how to differentiate good clay from bad. What had at first encounter been an apparent waste of time was, in fact, a masterclass in clay.

Similarly in the classroom there will be time for experiment and freedom but it will not be without purpose. It will be play 'with a purpose', to learn to know the medium. For those who would set up creative possibilities for children you must know your medium; as you shape it so it shapes you.
"When a child has to struggle to focus his attention on keeping a material under control, imaginative possibilities and aesthetic considerations take a back seat"

Finding the most suitable material to express your ideas can only come about as a result of building a repertoire of experiences with different media. There is a misunderstanding in schools about how this should be done. The idea that children should be presented with a vast array of materials as early as possible and from those experiences they will get to know the right one, is a nonsense. Nothing could be further from the truth. In essence, what this book seeks to establish is that whilst a wide range of materials could and perhaps should, in time be made available to young children, there are certain materials through which key experiences and practices can be provided which once learnt, establish an understanding which can be applied to other materials in due course.

It takes all of every day to develop the skills a young child needs to interpret those aspects of the world that excite them and interest them. That period of training time seems to be exactly right for Primary School children who need to find a limited number of media through which they can express and interpret their own ideas with confidence. The message for the child is:

## FIND THE BEST MEDIUM FOR YOU AND LEARN TO **CONTROL IT** for without technical skill freedom of expression is restricted

It goes without saying, that to be in control of whatever medium you choose is paramount and is a prerequisite for success. To continue the metaphor of the potter, when the clay is centred on the wheel, one can see and feel control and it is only then that freedom of expression can follow. The creative capacities of children are released or inhibited through the choice of medium they use and there is little chance of developing creativity if the only material on offer is screwed up tissue paper. Inadequate materials lead to trite means of expression and consequently teachers of young children must constantly search to:

## GIVE CHILDREN MATERIALS OF INTRINSIC WEALTH

So, just as creativity can be constrained or even suppressed by the wrong medium, so there have been many adults and children whose creativity has been initiated and inspired by a particular medium. In painting, it may be the first translucent marks with water colours in the nursery, in music the solitary tones of the oboe, in writing the lyric of rhyming words. In all creative processes the medium gives back as much, if not more than is put into it, if it is chosen carefully. Ideas flow between the two and once the mechanical mastery of the medium does not dominate its use, then creativity can begin to develop and flow naturally.

Skills which are well developed and repeatedly practised, in turn release creative potential.

Whilst I have indicated that imagination is an important part of creativity I am also aware that imagination on its own, in its own right needs a medium to give it substance. Whilst I might imagine something and keep it to myself, when I come to share it with you or anyone else, I need to do something to bring it into being. In order to create something each of us must find a medium, through which, within which, we can express our ideas. Sometimes young children are surrounded with the opportunities to explore different media and we frequently describe this exploration as play. Play is an important part of learning, not only because of its significance in language development and socialisation but also because it provides the child at school, sometimes for the first time, with the opportunity to find out "What happens if...?" Young children need the chance to explore a wide variety of materials to find out what they do, how they differ from one another and more importantly, how easy or difficult they are to control and manipulate.

Whilst it is important that the range of experiences of different media should be broad, too much too soon can lead to a butterfly behaviour, moving from activity to activity without any real sense of purpose. I have watched a young child in a Nursery pour sand, push a truck, empty beads onto the floor, paint a line on the table with someone else's brush, push another child over and spit at the goldfish! – all in ten minutes.

*Child - Year 4*

'Structured play' with a purpose is essential and the range of media needs to be carefully selected and new materials carefully introduced and presented. Over stimulation is almost as problematical to both teacher and learner, as the lack of it.

I believe that we should not provide a huge range of resources to be picked over at will, but should select them carefully and appropriately depending on the skills of the children and their disposition to learn. Children need to be successful with the medium they use in order to feel free to explore its full potential with confidence. Creativity can be suppressed, even destroyed by expecting children to apply themselves to a wrong or inappropriate medium. I watched a teacher encourage a group of children to look closely at a rose. She pointed out the shapes of the petals and how they were different from the shapes of the leaves, they noticed the stalk and the sharp thorns which grew from it, they savoured its smell and as they carefully passed it around from hand to hand, the word delicate was introduced by the teacher. "Now we're going to make one".

You can imagine my surprise when the children returned to their desks and opened a biscuit tin in which was a sludge coloured lump of rigid plasticene A less suitable material to make a rose, I had never seen.

The medium needs to be appropriate for the task and readily managed by the child, better still exciting to the child. There also needs to be a belief in the process communicated by the way the medium is provided. In the case of the plasticene, when the lesson ended whatever had been created was collected up in a lump and put back in the tin for next time! Creativity can be destroyed not only by the wrong media but also by the evident value placed on the enjoyment with it.

We all have examples in our own lives of friends or colleagues who come late to finding themselves through finding the right mediium. To be creative we need both the means and the skill and some people take a long time to acquire these, their experiences just have not given them the opportunity. The recently popular film, "Billy Elliot," set the world of the boy dancer in a social context, which showed the complex prejudices which surround aspects of the performing arts even today.

There are of course aspects of the arts which are less controversial than dance and whilst I believe that all children have a birthright to learn to dance and to learn about dance, like any other of the creative and performing arts, it cannot be successful unless the learners are disposed to it and the teachers value it. Dance is a medium of equal importance to painting and also a discipline which has a hierarchy of stages of development, which must be understood in order that the creative potential is not impeded. Learning to control the medium is of the utmost importance and teachers must be helped to have the insight and skills that enable this to happen.

I don't want to give the impression that children should not have the opportunity to explore and experiment with a range of media, in order to find the best fit. But, in order to achieve the very best, firstly we need to give children high quality materials in order to enhance their creative potential.

way the repertoire of marks provides the opportunity to describe the subject in a variety of ways. This is how very young children's drawings differ from older children's and there is a progression of skill development, which can be mapped out for both the teacher and the child. Learning to draw is a technical achievement as well as a cultural one, and the reason that many adults say they cannot draw is because, as children in school, they were allowed to believe they couldn't draw. They never had the opportunity to:

1.  become skilful at making a variety of marks;
2.  learn how these marks can be used to interpret an experience or subject;
    and
3.  at the watershed experience of the left and right brain dilemma, they have been dominated by left-brain teaching and learning strategies

Left brain behaviour which dominates many conventional teaching methods eliminates or dumbs down any likelihood of the learner taking these risks and experimenting with marks to represent ideas. Technical skills in drawing need to be developed alongside experimentation and it is only when these two complementary activities are operating alongside each other that creative drawing can develop.

As will be described later, those same principles can be applied every time a child or an adult seeks to find a way to interpret their experience. Of course in school, the carefully selected variety of choices given to the child at different stages of development gives opportunity for real creativity. It is of equal concern that these same creative learning behaviours are also present when children are working in subject disciplines, and it is readily evident in the best teaching of History, Geography and Science that these disciplines can be either taught and learnt creatively or limited to didactic and systematic methodologies.

I well remember as a student attending a lecture on time lines. A potentially dry subject was brought alive by the use a string across the room representing the previous two thousand years. The lecturer asked individual students to peg on to the line a series of cards representing key events (birth of Christ, Battle of Hastings, etc). As each event was fixed to the line, generally in time order, it became clear that no thought had to be given to the gaps between to represent 100 or 1000 years.

Formal education in the United Kingdom concentrated heavily on a narrow interpretation of 'literacy'. Children's ability to communicate using words is seen, quite rightly, as a key skill that will open up many different fields of experience and knowledge. Surprisingly, visual literacy and communication are less valued. Yet, throughout history, drawing has had a key place in the design of, say, a cathedral or Elizabethan war ship - drawings have helped the builders understand the structure and envisage the end product. We now live in an increasingly visual world. In the media, sounds and images are brought dynamically together. In print, words and pictures are more and more used in combination. The computer screen offers the possibility of manipulating images as readily as words.

Children need to be able to understand and manipulate both. The growing importance of visual media demands reconsideration of the importance of visual literacy and the learning methods and teaching strategies that will support its development.

Ruskin believed the main value of drawing is that it helps us to see.

**"...One day on the road to Norwood I noticed a bit of ivy round a thorn stem... and proceeded to make a pencil study of it in my grey paper pocket book, carefully, liking it more and more as I drew.  When it was done, I saw that I had  virtually lost all my time since I was twelve years old, because no one had ever told me to draw what was really there!...I had never seen the beauty of anything, not even of a stone – how much less a leaf!"**

 This is an entirely topical proposition: 'seeing intelligently' is high on the agenda for basic skills in the 21st century.  The development of film, television and digital media means that the world of ideas is more dominated by visual concepts and communications than ever before.  Being more confident with drawing will help young people engage with the contemporary world on their – and its own – terms.

# Developing The Skills & Routines

## "It takes seven years of rigorous training to be spontaneous in dance"

Isadora Duncan

Basic skills are frequently learnt in isolation to hone the use and practice of those skills. It is also evident, particularly from recent years of Literacy Strategy teaching, that in order to write with any purpose or sense of ownership, teachers need to stimulate the imagination of children. Clearly, there are two aspects which are interdependent and can be expressed in the following model:

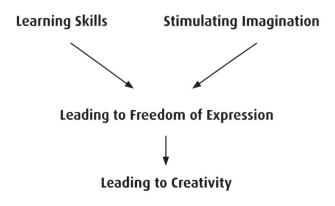

**Learning Skills**          **Stimulating Imagination**

**Leading to Freedom of Expression**

**Leading to Creativity**

I have made reference to teachers telling children to go away and use their imagination. This kind of direction is unlikely to be productive because it reveals a lack of understanding about how imagination is mastered and developed. It cannot be turned on like a tap with the expectation that imagination will consequently flow. Equally, the repetition of a skill, practising it, is very important but a child will not be enthused if the purpose and aims of the exercise are not clear. Skills practised in isolation are of little worth and are unlikely to be sustained or rehearsed with any purpose unless the learner can realise the possibilities which will arise as a result of mastering them.

This is true of skills in many disciplines be it sport, music, or for example, dance. The sustaining of the regular revisiting and practice, is the key to the mastery of the skill and teachers need to encourage the learner for the sustained efforts required in this, as they do in other forms of learning behaviours. Many adults know that they failed to learn to play a musical instrument because they were left alone to practice the skills, sometimes very basic ones, in isolation. Today we know that when these same skills are learnt with others and the activity itself is enjoyable, application is sustained. The best example of this is to watch children, sometimes very young, learning to play the violin using the Suzuki method of practice.

There are learning behaviours which must be understood by the teacher in order that the child can develop skills to a high level. As skills become more proficient the possibility of expression, using those skills becomes greater. As a series of skills is mastered, such as dance steps, so the potential of linking them together in an infinite number of ways becomes possible. **At the time when the skill becomes 'second nature' it has been mastered.** It is like a second skin and this enables the learner to be creative using that skill in conjunction with others that have been mastered in the same way.

As we observe children, it is readily evident that even from an early stage of development they "delight in tasks which they can perform with deftness and skill". (Handbook of Suggestions for Teachers 1937). I have listened to and watched children repeat skills apparently for the sake of it because they think they can do it. The embedding of skills and their rehearsal is a reassuring human behaviour and we all, even as adults, gain confidence and pride in repeating something we can do well.

# How was it for you?

In my secondary school, all boys were required to do woodwork if they were not clever enough to study a foreign language. I was not clever enough and each week visited a converted stable some distance from the main school complex, to study woodwork. The teaching was strict and any boy who misbehaved would be beaten with a length of wooden dowelling – in this way the teacher established his authority.

The largest part of our time was spent on learning how to make joints, joints being considered the most important skill in joining pieces of wood. This began painstakingly and slowly with the simplest processes and gradually progressed to the most complex methods. The wood used to practise the easiest joints was of poor quality, progressing to mahogany for the most difficult joints. The principle was fine except that some boys never progressed from the first simple joints. In fact, because their skills in cutting and planing the wood were so poor, they made little or no progress and the repetitive nature of the task became boring rather than an opportunity to practise a skill. In truth the only product of their hours of work were heaps of sawdust and wood shavings! This might be excusable except that the ultimate achievement was to make a secret dovetail - for some boys this took more than a term to complete, after having studied joints for four years!

Unfortunately I never achieved this level nor did any of my friends. I never had the chance to use the 'dovetailing' skills to make a piece of furniture. By the time I left school, the first signs of Multiple Density Fibreboard had entered the D.I.Y. market and the use of the dovetail disappeared with it, except in the hands of the master craftsmen restoring antiques or making bespoke furniture.

Skills which have no obvious purposeful application can be seen to be a futile experience. But experience which is meaningful has its own eternity.

## Developing a skill

### "Without technical skills freedom of expression is restricted"

It seems to me that creativity is as much to do with perspiration as inspiration. As in most fields of human activity there is an essential element of conscientious workmanlike application needed to capitalize on an initial idea or ambition. But before I develop that idea, I also want to introduce the notion of knowing that something is right for you, a sort of sixth sense; and of course the opposite feeling that something is not suited to you.

In our perceptions of the world around us, there are times when all of us feel an experience or activity as being good and rewarding in its own right. At such moments the learner doesn't need a teacher to tell them whether what they have done is good, very good or no good – it is irrelevant because we know it 'within ourselves'. We have other phrases which readily spring to mind such as, 'feeling at ease with', 'fit for the purpose, 'in your element'. For the developing child searching to find ways to interpret experience is very important since when a particular pattern of behaviour feels right, it tends to be repeated and other modes of behaviour become associated with it. By building a repertoire of 'feel right' behaviours the opportunity to pick up bad behaviours by chance recedes.

With very young children it is very important to recognise when they are behaving intuitively and developing a level of skill. Throughout the processes of all worthwhile learning, learning in the sense of acquiring a skill (playing an instrument, doing a handstand, focusing a microscope), care, control and technique go hand in hand and achievement is never the result of combining behaviours which are awkward or lacking purpose in their own right. In order to do anything with skill and dexterity one must discover for oneself, the right feeling.

**"The hand when it holds a tool is an instrument of discovery. Lace a shoe, thread a needle, play a recorder, fly a kite. The hand is the cutting edge of the mind. The progress of learning is the refinement of the hand in action"**

Bronowski

I watched my four-year-old granddaughter learning to ride a two-wheeled bicycle, a skill which her brother, more than a year older, had just learnt. She set off and fell off but was determined to succeed. She didn't want stabilisers and eventually allowed my reassuring hand to hold the seat as I ran alongside her. All my worries were about steering, stopping and falling off – she was solely concerned with balance. She fell off many times on the first day until she wearied of the task. The next day she began again and I followed. Suddenly she shouted, "Let go – let go." - I did and she fell off. She climbed back on, rejected my help, set herself up and rode away – she had found her balance! Minutes later she ran into a tree! She now had to learn how to look where she was going and how to stop.

**"The pianist who concentrates solely on his fingers can paralyse himself"**

Polyani

In developing a skill, there is unity in the activity itself and there are also a number of other factors which impinge on potential success. A conscious analysis of what we are doing can sometimes interrupt the action, causing failure. In contrast there are times when we use this very method to help us recall something which we find difficult to store in the memory. For example, facts which are difficult to memorize can be embodied in rhymes, and some people have the capacity for remembering seemingly endless series of figures which they fit to a rhyme. Such 'tricks' which we call mnemonics, are only the conscious application of what is an unconscious principle of growth and adaptation. Balance and symmetry, proportion, rhythm and harmony are fundamental factors of aesthetic experience. Indeed, they are the only elements by means of which experience can be organized into persisting patterns, and it is of their nature that they imply fluency, economy and efficiency.

What works right, feels right; and the result, for the individual, is that heightening of the senses which is essential for creativity to grow. "I can't draw, I don't like dancing, I can't stand on one leg, clay is messy, who wants to paint anyway and as for music, who'd want to play the guitar – not me, I can't even sing". All such excuses offered at different times in response to the opportunity to learn a skill. "I can't", is a way of saying "I'm embarrassed about my inability to even make a start and rather than feel foolish, I won't expose myself to that kind of experience because it's uncomfortable". In other words, "I don't know how".

The possibility of the development of any aspect of creative potential is thwarted from the outset in these circumstances and the experienced teacher sets out deliberately in the teaching of skills by starting where the child is, rather than where they should be. Creative achievement is proportionally related to the control of the medium, the greater the control the greater the creative potential. But we have to remember, as I pointed out earlier, that many children spend hours, even days, learning skills which are useless, have little or no application or are never used once acquired.

## "When a child has to struggle to focus his attention on keeping a material under control, imaginative and aesthetic considerations take a back seat"

Eisner

Learning a skill, say beating a drum, is one step along the path to becoming a drummer. The best teaching will allow time for experimentation to tap and beat the drum in a whole variety of ways and as the excitement of exploration fades, one short sound pattern will be chosen and then repeated. It is of course possible to develop a level of proficiency in drumming and simultaneously destroy any enjoyment for the potential drummer. There is a balance therefore between acquiring skills and being stimulated, even inspired, to explore possibilities.

Teaching a range of skills which help children to respond to their experiences is of course a fundamental principle of good Primary education. In all the best schools there is also an emphasis on training children to adopt a disciplined approach to tools and materials so that no one comes to commence an activity to find tools or resources out of place, dirty or spoiled.

## "We always put the things we use, back, ready for the next person to choose"

Girl aged 8

The growth of manipulative skill and competence takes time and steady application; it is never achieved if pupils are introduced to a myriad of tools and practices and left to get on with it. If children are expected to change from one process to another too often, their level of engagement and application will become superficial. Steady and consistent routines and practice in time breed the confidence that comes through mastery and empathy with the world of tools and materials.

## "The way in which materials are presented is as important as the materials themselves"

It is important to emphasise again here how selection and choice are important elements in building the child's confidence in the control of the medium and its appropriateness for the interpretation of an experience. Too wide a choice can lead to bewilderment and despair in selecting and rejecting the resources best suited to the task. There are clearly inexpensive tools and resources which can be made readily available to all children. But, I believe that for the majority of schools which I have worked with over the last twenty years, there is a need to establish a hierarchy of what is desirable, of the greatest relevance and use and at the outset, which can be started relatively easily.

The child needs to find ways to hold on to numerous and diverse experiences and make the best of them. I have indicated that I believe that this is best done through teaching children to observe closely and carefully and giving them time to contemplate in so doing. I have now introduced a way of achieving this – the development of skills needed to interpret their observations and thoughts to turn them into something concrete, because being creative involves doing something, bringing something into being, which wasn't there before.

In order that this can happen using the principles I have introduced so far, the child or the adult who is given the opportunity to be creative, can't be looking over their shoulder to see if what they are doing, or thinking of doing, is what is deemed correct or pleasing to the teacher. Whilst praise from any teacher will give reassurance and raise self-esteem, it is not the critical characteristic at the launch point of creating something for yourself. It is equally futile to copy someone else, which of course may suggest that you either don't understand what you are doing or don't have any ideas in your head.

Alan Ashley Pitt summarises the dilemma when he writes:

## "The man who follows the crowd will usually get no further than the crowd.

## The man who walks alone is likely to find himself in places no-one has ever been before"

What we are talking about here is 'going it alone', being comfortable with oneself and one's own ideas, 'stepping into the dark', exploring the unknown in order to broaden the opportunity to make new connections and generate new ideas. It's about taking risks. Perhaps, as a statement, this is too raw and I need to redefine it in a more forceful way.

## "If you want to see the stars you have to venture out into the dark"

So the challenge lies in creating a workplace where children and people can be the best they can be. They need to be stimulated because of their experiences, have had the time to assimilate them, have the appropriate materials or opportunity to interpret them and the skill to be able to control both themselves and their chosen medium. Lastly then, we want all learners with these prerequisites in place, to reach out beyond the immediate and the obvious to find their own original means of expression.

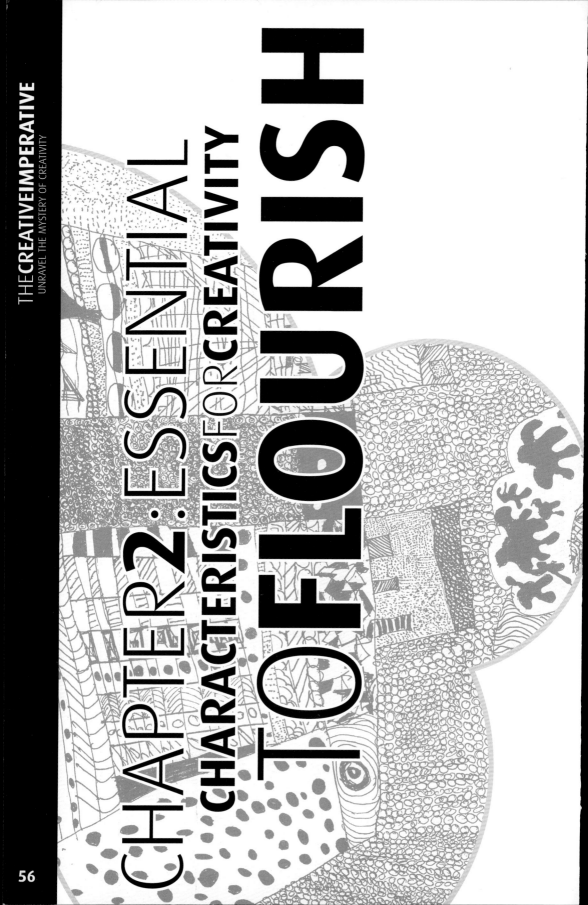

# CHAPTER 2: ESSENTIAL CHARACTERISTICS FOR CREATIVITY TO FLOURISH

# CHAPTER 2: Characteristics For Creativity to Flourish

## EXPERIENCE

"Experience is not constituted merely by the succession of events themselves. A person can be witness to a tremendous parade of episodes and yet, if he fails to make something out of them, or if he waits until they have all occurred before he attempts to reconstrue them, he gains little in the way of experience from having been around when they happened"

A Theory of Personality – G Kelly 1963, p.73

This quotation which introduces the next part of the book is chosen carefully. Throughout our lives it is the experiences which we have which shape us and cause us to become the kind of people we are. Meaningful experiences do stay with us and in a sense last for ever. We are able to recall them in different ways and over a period of time we revisit them, share them with others, elaborate on them or even imaginatively reconstruct them. We can have such intense recall of them that they almost recur. The most important experiences last throughout our lives and even the lives of others who shared the experience with us. It is quite clear that no one can have an experience for us or on our behalf. They might have the same experience at exactly the same moment but their responses to it and memories of it may be totally different to ours. Take, for example, an audience listening to an orchestra playing the 2nd movement of a Beethoven Concerto. Everyone hears the same instruments making the same sounds but we cannot know how many of the audience, if any, are having similar or the same experiences as we are.

For children, experiences come in many forms every moment of their lives. Depending on the kinds of experiences they have, so their capacity to build schemata from those experiences is determined. The child's creative potential is influenced by the construction of these schemata, their active knowledge which builds up and gives shape to their ideas. Generally, children develop their schemata of an experience until it is consolidated and during that process the idea becomes more formalised.

As a little girl, my grand daughter had a pony. She drew horses and ponies all the time and every time she created a picture she wanted to include one. At first she asked lots of questions about the legs, the head, the position of the ears, the length of the tail. She then progressed to putting herself on the horse and was concerned with details about herself relating to the horse, her riding hat, the stirrups, her pony-tail. Gradually, the questions were less, the drawing became formalised and whenever she drew a picture, even of the seaside, she included herself on a horse and completed the task quickly and easily. She subsequently repeated the same process when describing herself and a favourite pony in clay and quickly arrived at a form which satisfied her.

All the time, new aspects and details of her experiences modified her interpretation and sometimes altered it. As she moved on to consider and interpret other experiences, the horse and rider schemata were 'so to speak', stored and could be brought out to be added to or modified at any time or just used as part of another experience.

I shall develop these ideas about schemata later, but firstly it is necessary to explore the nature of experience more fully.

*Child - Year 2. Translating ideas into three dimensional form develops understanding.*

The environment, the world in which the child lives, provides the raw material for experience. Raw may be exactly the word we need when considering the different kinds of experiences children may have. Obviously, some experiences may also be rich. We cannot and should not seek to protect children from the raw in order to replace it with the rich but a diet of one kind of experience to the detriment of the other, presents an imbalance of experience which is not a true reflection of the world in which we live.

a newly born family of day-old kittens, all with their eyes still closed. On a close-up, the commentary explained that all kittens have their eyes closed when born and although they are not very lively when asleep, they will soon change. The commentary then explained that unfortunately, one was dead. My granddaughter became quite distraught and started to cry, her brother consoled her by saying – 'they're only pretending'.

Some experiences really are first hand – whilst others have been processed, in this case, by the media and my grandson! The important point here is that the symbols that children use to express their understanding of these experiences are drawn from many varied and diverse sources.

So in Picasso's terminology, the child is **"the receptacle of emotions and experiences from no matter where; from the sky, from the earth, a piece of paper, a passing figure, a cobweb".**

If we now continue this line of thought and develop it, it is quite obvious how the kinds of experiences which shape children's lives outside school are all important. It also goes without saying that for those whose lives are so contained that they have very limited experience, their opportunities in school to respond creatively to questions presented by the teacher, are likely to be very limited.

**"Experience is never limited and it is never complete. It is an immense sensibility, a kind of huge spider's web of the finest silken threads suspended in the chamber of consciousness, and catching every airborne particle in its tissue"**

So the contemporary child has the potential for enormous enrichment as a result of being born in the twenty-first century. Their world is no longer limited by their own physical contact with it, it embraces the whole world through the many sophisticated communication systems which surround us all.

A word of explanation is perhaps also needed here, in order to realise how opportunities change in the kind of experiences already referred to.

My grandfather lived in Colchester for most of his life and I can remember when we visited him how he liked to walk in the town and show us alterations that had been made to shops and roads since our previous visit. We seemed to spend hours admiring all the plants and vegetables in his garden and on his two allotments!! He and my grandmother could never eat the produce of so much horticulture and he gave most of it to friends and neighbours. His whole life was bound up in Colchester, his work, his family and his gardening. He returned from work and as a present, to help him get to his two allotments, which were more than a mile away, more easily, my grandmother bought him a bicycle.

In hindsight, it was the worst thing she ever did. To begin with it did help him to get to the allotments more quickly but within two years they were totally overgrown and his garden at home looked unkempt. Why? He found he could travel and so set out to discover the world of Essex, which previously had only existed as an idea. Within two years he had visited over sixty churches, followed rivers and railway lines, discovered forests, farms and animals that had never been part of his experiences. He was so enthralled by his new opportunities for travel that he purchased a primus stove in a metal box which he fixed to the back of the cycle seat, so that he could make hot drinks in the winter months of his travelling and discovery.

My grandmother became a lonely lady. She couldn't go with him, indeed wouldn't, when he suggested he would buy a tandem! She made his sandwiches before going to bed each night, since he frequently left home at daybreak, always returning before dark.

When we visited him in his later years, he spent hours in the evenings showing me the drawings he had made and scribbled notes he had written, recording every detail of his experiences.

**"I don't know what I may seem to the world, but, as to myself, I seem to have been only like a boy playing on the sea shore and divesting myself, now and then finding a smoother pebble or a prettier shell than ordinary, whilst the great ocean of truth lay all undiscovered before me"**

Isaac Newton

How different is the child's world today! I was sixteen before I left Britain to visit a foreign country, but both my grandchildren had been abroad several times before they were five! If it is true that our experiences shape us to become what we are, what potential is there in every classroom waiting to be harnessed. There are many children who are fortunate enough to have parents who can provide the breadth and richness of experience which gives children the opportunities to express their feelings, emotions and responses in a variety of ways. It is also clear that if a child is going to link one experience to another in order that more complex ideas can be developed through the association of ideas from different experiences; then quality experiences count. Of equal interest and importance is that we depend on our real experiences to help us to give greater meaning and depth to our imagined experience. Therefore, it is very important for teachers to realize that the richer our realization, structuring and interpretation of our real experiences, the richer will be the potential of our imagination. This principle is of the utmost importance in developing creativity in primary education. Commenting on his first flight into space an American astronaut said, "What is accepted fact today, was only once just imagined".

It is worth noting at this point how this principle is illustrated in, for example, children's drawings where, although the subject of a drawing may be imaginary, the detail of its content is dependent on the child's knowledge of the world which surrounds him. . As we have already seen in Chapter 1, the child brings to the task of imagining, all his active knowledge about animals, in order to 'create' a monster. His schemata are built on, modified and altered as a result of developing experiences, for example, seeing another child move like a monster, listening to a piece of writing or the first lines of a poem about a monster as well as his own observations of a variety of animals.

**"Flared nostrils fumed the temper in his dazzling eyes. Dagger-fanged teeth imprisoned the terror cries"**

Boy aged 9

Whatever the product of these kinds of opportunities, it is clear that for a large number of children, insufficient depth and richness of experience outside school limits their opportunity to express ideas inside school and subsequently limits their potential creativity. What the teacher is obviously striving to do is to help each child to organise and internalise their own experiences so that they can draw on them as and when necessary. The most important way in which this is done in the best schools and by the best teachers, is through a close study of the kinds of experiences children have outside school and then to design a range of experiences to build on that inside school, ie through the curriculum. This simple statement assumes so much and against a background in the late 1990's of a prescriptive curriculum, it seems an absurd statement. Let me put it another way:

**"Knowledge that is not founded in experience will not keep any better than wet fish"**

If it doesn't say in the National Curriculum that you should study cats, and you had a class of children, (most unlikely) none of whom had ever seen a cat, would you ignore that lack of experience, compensate for it or reject the idea because there was no directive to do so? From the outset of the National Curriculum the wisest teachers have used its best characteristics as guidelines and built on them. In other words, they have examined recommended areas of study in any subject and where appropriate, used the guidance and made it relevant to the school's particular circumstances.

It is the teacher, and only the teacher, who has the insight into the experiences of a particular class of children. What should be appropriate and what is, are frequently not the same thing. Consequently, choosing rich and meaningful experiences in school for children and then shaping the way those experiences take place is as important, if not more important for some children, as what takes place outside school.

It would seem from this chapter so far, that I am suggesting that experience is everything and indeed that could be true. We do indeed learn through experience but we do not learn by merely being exposed to it. In Christian Schiller's words: "Like a flash photograph"

**"Learning comes when we turn over an experience in our mind; we begin to think about it, and usually we want to tell somebody about it – a friend – to explain, relive it, digest it, until it has become part of ourselves, lasting forever. All lasting learning is a becoming."**

If children, and subsequently adults, are the product of their experience and they learn through that experience, the implications on creative potential are significant. If we want children to be innovative, to take intellectual risks and to make new connections between things which are, at first sight, not obvious, then the way we shape or cause the experience to happen will also have a great deal to do with our appreciation of the nature of the child and his developing experiences.

**"It is familiarity with life that makes time speed quickly. When every day is a step into the unknown, as for children, the days are long with the gathering of experience"**

George Gissing

**To create these conditions, schools should:**

- create a school environment where learning is initiated through the children's relationships with the world around them.

- recognise the uniqueness of that relationship. Children frequently gain intense personal delight in things which appear to adults of little or no consequence.

- build on our experiences sequentially. That is not to say that experiences must be so arranged as to arrive in the right order - life is not like that! But the relevance of an experience is frequently greater if it can be associated or linked to an earlier one. It could be argued therefore, that teachers arrange experiences developmentally for children as is appropriate to their need. (know a cat, before you meet a tiger)

- recognise that scale is important. Surrounded by a "multicoloured media swap-shop", many children need to be helped to select out from the myriad of experiences around them, to concentrate the focus of their attention on the specific

- complement whatever the experiences are outside school. The experiences within school will be so arranged as to 'catch children up' in experiences which fascinate them and in turn, relate to and broaden their experiences outside the classroom.

· from a very early age, enable children to build up a wealth of sensory appreciation, Sights, Sounds, Smells, Tastes and Textures. All help to shape the understanding.

**"The most important thing you can learn by experience is the thing you didn't learn by experience"**

# SCHEMATA

## "Every child has its own Schemata"

Herbert Read

More than a hundred year ago James Sully published his studies in childhood (1895). He was one of the leading psychologists of the day and became very interested in children's drawings and their significance. Sully noted the various stages in the development of children's drawings, starting with what appeared to be aimless scribble leading to the sophisticated symbols used by six year-olds to describe their experiences in the world around them. Cyril Bennett in his Spatial and Scholastic Tests (Pages 319-322) later identified the stages of development more closely and between the ages of five to eight he identifies two categories – Descriptive Symbolism and Descriptive Realism.

### Descriptive Symbolism – age 5 to 6

"Human figure now reproduced with tolerable accuracy, but as a crude symbolic schema. The features are localized in the roughest way and each is a conventional form. The general 'schema' assumes a somewhat different type with different children, but the same child clings pretty closely, for most purposes and for long periods, to the same favourite pattern".

### Descriptive Realism – age 7 to 8

"The drawings are still logical rather than visual. The child 'sets down' what he knows, not what he sees; and is still thinking, not of the present individual, but rather of the generic type'. He is trying to communicate, express, or catalogue all that he remembers, or all that interests him, in a subject. The 'schema' becomes more true to detail; items, however, are suggested more by association of ideas than by the analysis of percept. Profile views of the face are attempted, but perspective, opacity, foreshortening, and all the consequences of singleness of viewpoint are still disregarded. There is a gathering of interest in decorative detail".

The **schema** is a formula, a kind of shorthand used by the child to describe what he or she actively knows about the subject and as I have already described, the child stays with and repeats schema sometimes for many months until new realizations modify or change it. The reason for wanting to focus so closely on this apparently inconsequential aspect of child development will now be evident in the light of the previous pages describing the importance of experience.

As we build some clear idea of how creativity is developed and taught, it is obvious that every child needs to develop a wide range of symbols to interpret their experience. If those symbols are going to grow, develop and change, if there is going to be a desire to communicate their changing understandings of the world around them and what they've noticed, then the kind of experiences children are given in school are of the utmost importance.

Symbols fill our lives. The easiest one to describe is probably ***(an asterisk)***. By making such a mark on a page, the reader knows by conventions in the written word that I intend to draw your attention to something outside the normal run of the text on this page; to, for example, a footnote. The symbol stands for a directive; please look at the Footnote at the bottom of the page.

Other symbols surround us daily to communicate immediately where words would be too cumbersome or complicated. Road

* **Footnote at the bottom of the page**

signs are a simple example – the symbols or signs used for level crossings, double bends or animals likely to be crossing the road ahead are a more immediate means of communicating than words. Road signs are not, however, universal. There has not been a worldwide agreement on the symbols which should be used – indeed, there may never be and it is perhaps undesirable that there should be. But if you saw a building which had a cross on it, anywhere in the world, you would know that the building has been or is associated with the Christian religion - a very simple symbol for what is a vast complexity of images and ideas.

Anything can be a symbol. A flower can be a symbol of love, sad or happy recollections. Flowers have different personal associations for different people and of course, there are many different species of flowers. These kinds of symbols are very personal, whereas the formal symbols of, for example, the asterisk or the cross are intended to mean something.

Words and numbers are symbols too, only they are different since they are **systematic symbols**. The asterisk was the earlier example. It, like all systematic symbols is governed by a set of rules and there is an agreed set of procedures as to how and when it is used. Words and numbers respectively have meanings and values. There are ways that children can check what a word means, how it is spelt and in good dictionaries how it can be used – it conforms to a set of rules for its application and use. Similarly with numbers, they too follow procedures which can be learnt. Our number system is based on the ten Arabic numerals from 0 to 9, which when combined in different ways and following agreed procedures, realize a prescribed set of expectations. Working out what a word means or how big or small a number is and its value, is not a hit and miss process, it is systematic.

In contrast but complementary to it we have **schematic symbols,** which can be found most readily, for example, in painting, poetry, music, drama or dance. Understanding schematic symbols and their use is for many people at the crux of understanding the nature of creativity itself. Music is composed in notation, plays are written in words. The musical score is not the music just as the written words on the page, the text, are not the play. The music and the play are written in the schematic form but are dependent on musicians or actors interpreting the sounds and words, thus giving them shape and meaning. If it were possible, we should now listen to two different interpretations of the same musical score, for example, the Benjamin Britten 'Sea Symphony', then watch and listen to two different groups of actors interpreting a scene from a Shakespeare play, for example, Act Two, Scene One of A Midsummer Night's Dream. It is therefore not surprising that almost every year a different group of actors with a different producer announce a "totally new interpretation of a particular play". The actors are trying to capture, describe and portray the qualities and characteristics, which they feel best typify the characters they represent in the circumstances in which they are portrayed. Their interpretation is unique.

In music, of course, the sound produced by the orchestra, band or group is governed by exactly the same principles. The musicians give a form to the music by the way they interpret and respond both to each other and together and like the actors, no two performances are identical, even though they follow the same score and notation. The poet and the dancer equally are seeking to capture and express the essential characteristics and qualities of an experience. Each of these forms of expression allows us the opportunity to build our responses, note by note, line by line or step by step, we interpret what we see as the play, the dance or the concerto unfolding in front of us.

We respond to it in two different but complementary ways, which are unique to schematic symbols:

(a)  Line by line, step by step, note by note.

**OR**

(b)  Considering the performance as a whole when the curtain falls, the dance is complete or the last note is played.  We make sense of it, each for ourselves, from the totality of the experience.

So as audience we can and do respond to the total experience. All the parts have come together to make the whole.  As we have been watching and listening, we have responded to what is being expressed, but when it is over our applause is recognition of the achievement of the play or concert as a whole, what has been expressed "in the play" and "by the play".

Painting is not quite the same.  The audience does not applaud in front of a painting say, for example, at the Tate Gallery.  It is seldom that we have the opportunity, as with music, to watch the different parts unfold, although earlier I described in chapter 1 how Picasso had done this through film and how we had responded as the audience.  How then does the audience for a painting, the viewer, come to conclusions about how good a painting is.  There is no book of rules which the painter has followed, which will guide the viewer as to the arrangement and use of complementary or contrasting colour or a dictionary of meanings for the symbolic forms used in the painting.

Consider this painting by Marc Chagall and how you respond to it, like it or dislike it.  There is no right or wrong response and even though Chagall was an amazing artist of great talent,

*Green Violinist by Chargill*

whose imagination goes far beyond many of his contemporaries, it doesn't mean that you will automatically like his pictures.

In exactly the same way there is no guide book to tell us what Beethoven's fifth symphony is about, as there is no manual to help us decipher what a play means. We can of course, have books which describe what the author thinks different aspects of a play, painting or overture are about, but in the final analysis it is up to us to respond to what has been created in our own particular way. Each of these experiences is unique and the associations which take place between the actors, musicians or painting never occur again in exactly the same form. The feeling, response, which a work of art generates brings together not only what the work means, but how it is.

**Some years ago I visited the Royal Academy Summer Exhibition with a doctor friend. He was a person who**

collected watercolours, went to concerts and the theatre and was, to coin a phrase, 'well read'. He followed me from room to room in the exhibition muttering and interrupting my viewing with derogatory statements; 'a child could do better", 'they call that art?', 'I've never seen such rubbish'.

In room after room he continued to dismiss the work until I suggested to him that he go away and look at the pictures on his own because he was spoiling it for me. He curtly replied that he would go and wait at the entrance and he'd meet me there in an hour. At the appointed time he was nowhere to be found. For about twenty minutes I waited for him in vain and decided to go back in to the exhibition and see if he was there.

Eventually I found him sitting motionless in front of a painting. As I approached he didn't notice me. Reaching him I began "I thought we were supposed to be....." and then I stopped. He was crying! He just grabbed my arm and took me to the picture he was transfixed by. "Just look", he said, "I can't believe it". He was shaking. "I've never felt so emotional about a painting in my life – I didn't know you could".

If I reproduced the painting here, many would wonder what all the fuss was about, some might say, "I've never seen such rubbish!" The unique relationship between the artist and my friend is an example of how the complex symbols created out of an understanding of colour, shape and form communicated feelings born through experience.

The artist, the dancer, the poet, the musician, the writer try to capture the unique qualities of an experience. The creativity comes through the choices made from a wealth of experiences or from one experience which lends itself to best express an idea.

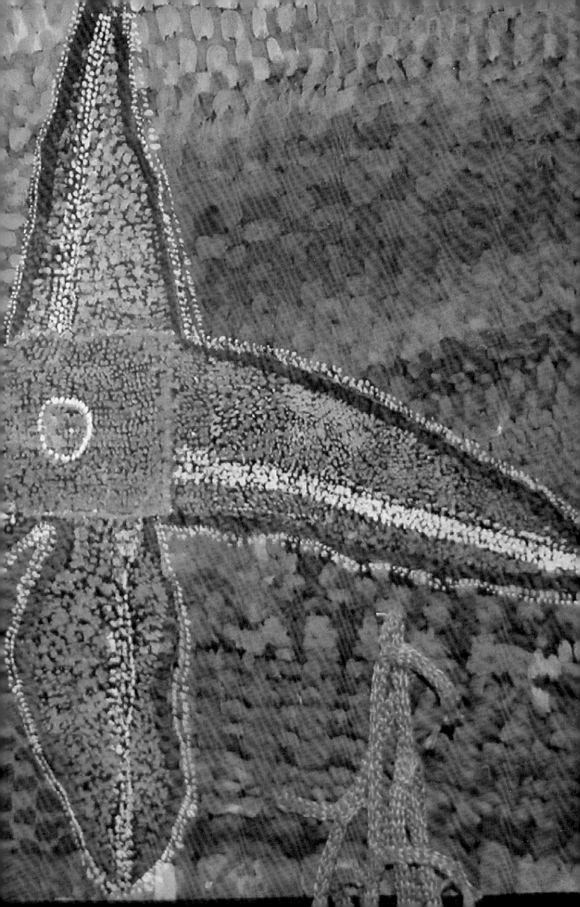

# CHAPTER **3**: BRIDGING **THE** LEARNING **GAP**

# CHAPTER**3**: **Bridging The Learning Gap**

## THE BRAIN

"We start with a foetus, which is like a blind kind of light without sense or intellect, and that struggles forward to become the kind of person with the kind of brain and intellect we possess.  Most of that process is taking place from the pre natal period until three years after birth, and from that moment on the apparatus for learning is there. Recent research in neurology is beginning to teach us that a lot of our gifts are innate and there for some kind of exploitation, but what is innate disappears and withers away in a very literal sense, nerve cells disappearing and ceasing to be available, if they are not consolidated by actual experience".

John Davies Emeritus Professor Paediatrics – Cambridge University 1994

## Lop Sided Brains

What Davies leaves us with in this statement is the idea of a huge brain potential awaiting stimuli through experience.  There are many books currently available which explore aspects of what is known about how the brain grows and develops – that knowledge is developing and changing daily.  What is constant in all of this is the central importance of experience and how it shapes the growing brain in every child.

So the kind of experiences children have shapes the kind of brain they develop and have for the rest of their lives.  They are in fact 'stuck with it', because they cannot go back later and change it! As a consequence, we have phrases in education such as, **"We are the product of our experiences"**.

Since so much of this book is about the kind of experiences we provide for children, it seems only right and proper that some attention should be given to better understand the relationship between the experience and the brain's response to it. Why? Because it would be particularly important to the planning of any educational development programme to know whether we are talking about just any old experience or whether there are some experiences which are very significant and without them we might have children who develop lop-sided brains or brains which cannot function properly because they have not been fully developed.

Davies also warns us of one other danger which I will come to later; the idea that brain cells which are not stimulated in the formative period of a child's development, wither away and are never available again. To me this inevitably brings about a necessity to know just what is going on inside the heads of children as we, as teachers or parents, determine the kind of experiences we give our children.

What is known is that the brain grows and changes in every human foetus as the child develops, comes into the world and begins its life. All normal brains at birth are physically the same in human beings and as the brain develops it produces trillions of cells, which in turn are the foundation for a multi trillion network of potential connections. We know that the networks of connections between different cells in the brain are brought about by the uses that are made of them. From the very earliest stages of development, within twenty-four hours of fertilization, DNA from the mother and father combines to form a new cell and this cell then subdivides and so the process of cell multiplication begins. As the process of subdivision gathers momentum, new cells migrate to positions throughout the central nervous system. Some of them become the basic cellular unit in the brain and are called **neurons** whilst others, known as **glia**, provide structure and nourishment to the developing neural network. Once new cells have migrated into the central nervous system, they, in turn, send out **dendrites** and **axons** to build up the brain's vast interconnecting network.

## The Structure

Each basic cellular unit in the brain is called a neuron, this creates a series of fibres which extend out from the cell body like tentacles. It is through these tentacles that the cell communicates and makes connections and the size and quality of the tentacles is determined by the frequency of their use. The main tentacles from the neuron, its main line of communication, are called **axons** and as it becomes frequently used it is coated with a protective sheath called **myelin.** The myelination of axons makes them more efficient.

The other tentacles, which the neuron creates, act as receptors, which receive chemical and electrical signals from other neurons, and this is where the most interesting part of the brain's developing complexity lies.

The neuron sends out its signals down the axon to the axon terminals. A receiving neuron has dendrites waiting to receive these signals and there is a gap between the two. Bridging that gap is a critical activity in brain development.

When **axons** reach the right **dendrites,** they form **synapses** - on the one side receptors from the dendrites, on the other impulses or signals from the axon. Between them are molecules, which are known as neuro-transmitters, and they enable the electrical impulses to be changed to channel impulses. If the impulse is strong enough and enduring enough it bridges the synaptic gap and is passed on to the next neuron. Its strength is of particular importance since a single neuron can build thousands of synapses, which in turn may mean many trillions of interconnections between neurons.

At birth a newborn baby has all its potential neurons in place to enable it to respond to the stimuli of the world which surrounds it. This is its experience, and, for example, from day one it can respond to visual stimuli. So as a baby grows it not only responds to external stimuli but there are periods in its development particularly in the early stages, when it needs to be exposed to sensory experiences - sight, sound, touch, taste, smell – in order to build the appropriate connections in the brain.

**How does it all work?**

The nature of our senses determines our field of perception, what we can perceive and how. Human beings have very different sensory perception potentials compared with other animals, for example sound. Many of us have dogs as pets – we share the same environment but are equipped differently to cope with it. Many dogs can hear sounds which humans cannot hear, have a highly developed sense of smell and taste and can see as well, if not better than humans. They respond to their sensory experiences, those that are relevant to them, in a different way to humans. If humans were more sensitive, for example, if we could smell with the same sensitivity as a dog, our lives would be changed significantly but our lives would be changed more radically and our perceptions totally altered if we could fly! The way we are constructed, our physical make-up determines our capacity and sensitivity to respond to the world around us.

It therefore follows that our brain cells are primed to respond to sensory experiences and the more of those experiences that the brain has, through exposure to experience and the repetition of them, the more the cells adapt and become better and stronger in their response. What is now becoming clear relates back to John Davies's original statement, the brain is responding to external stimuli and gets better and better at discerning, identifying and differentiating between, for example sounds, tastes and smells. So the brain develops to become the kind of brain you have as a direct result of the uses to which it has been put. It goes without saying that if it has been put to little use, not stimulated and kept in a sterile environment it is unlikely to develop its full potential.

I referred earlier to the connections being made in the brain and the importance of the bridging mechanism of the synapse. The density of synapses, their proliferation is at its highest in early childhood, millions of connections are being made every minute, every day and this process is known as 'synaptogenesis'. Up to the age of ten, children's brains contain more synapses than at any other time in their lives. Early childhood experiences fine-tune the brain's synaptic connections. In a process that we might describe as synaptic pruning, childhood experiences reinforce and maintain synapses that are repeatedly used, but snip away the unused synapses. Thus, this time of high synaptic density and experiential fine-tuning is a critical period in a child's cognitive development. It is the time when the brain is particularly efficient in acquiring and learning a range of skills. During this critical period, children can benefit most from rich, stimulating learning environments. If, during this critical period we deprive children of such environments, significant learning opportunities are lost forever.

Therefore, **"with the right input at the right time almost anything is possible"**, but if this window of opportunity is missed, the growing child is handicapped. Perhaps Jerome Bruner was actually correct to claim that "any subject can be taught effectively in some intellectually honest form to any child at any stage of development". The claim that children are capable of learning more at a very early age, when they have excess synapses and peak brain activity, is one of the more common ones made in neuroscience. Neuroscience implies that if information is presented in ways that fit each child's learning style, children are capable of learning more than is currently believed. On this same evidence, others urge that children begin the study of languages, advanced mathematics, logic and music as early as possible, possibly as early as age three or four. Parents should realize that they have a:

**"golden opportunity to mould a child's brain. And that calls for a full-court press during the early years   - that is, a rich child-care environment without undue academic stress".**

(Viadero, 1996, p32).

Ideally parents should become deeply involved in their children's early education because when brain activity is high, parents have a unique opportunity to foster a love of learning.

This process of synaptic proliferation, synaptogenesis, continues over a period of months that varies among different species. As I have already described, this period of synaptic over-production is followed by a period of synaptic elimination or pruning. This experience-dependent pruning process, which occurs over a period of years, reduces the overall number of synaptic connections to adult, mature levels, usually about the time of sexual maturity. The mature nervous system has fewer synaptic connections than were present during the development peak. It is the pattern, rather than simply the number of these connections that form the mature brain's neural circuitry and that supports normal brain function and therefore determines the kind of people we become.

## Who we become

**"As the brain is shaped in this way it follows that the kinds of stimuli we receive are of critical importance in shaping us to be the kind of people we become.**

**As we build networks – patterns of synaptic patterns when very young, so we build the framework which will shape how we learn as we get older: such shaping will significantly determine what we learn – it will be both an opportunity and a constraint. The broader and more diverse the experience when very young, the greater are the chances that, later in life, the individual will be able to handle open, ambiguous, uncertain and novel situations."**

Quoted by John Abbott from Quartz and Sejnowski. The Salk Institute. The Neural basis for cognitive development, a constructivist manifesto.

What is clear now is that the brain depends on experiences in order to build its networks. In order to respond to those experiences all the senses are deployed and each and every one plays an equally important part. This process is one of growth and development which is essential in coming to know the world. For example, seeing is not simply a question of passively recording information. We can only know the world through interaction with it and the absence of recognition or use of any one faculty can bring about an imbalance in potential which may never be rectified.

Dr Oliver Sachs the internationally known neurologist had a patient whom he chose to call Virgil. He had been blind from birth and as a result of an operation he regained his sight at fifty years of age.

People thought it would be a simple matter. They thought the operation to remove cataracts would either work or it wouldn't work, and if it worked he would be a sighted man and he would go out into the world and recognise it all and be like the rest of us. It was a few days after the operation that I got a call saying, 'Yes, he sees, but he doesn't know what he's seeing. What's happening?' So I went down to see him and he was obviously having the greatest difficulties. He described how, when the bandage came off 24 hours after surgery, he saw colours moving around and a sort of chaos, and out of this chaos there came a voice, the voice of his surgeon. And he said to himself: voices come from faces. This chaos – this must be a face.

Well I took him to the zoo and he was particularly eager to see the great apes, and one wondered whether he would recognise these. At first he didn't see anything. But it so happened that there was a great bronze statue of a gorilla there, and I asked him if he would like to examine this. And as he did so, his expertness and his skill and his confidence came back. He felt this animal lovingly and accurately, very swiftly – you could see what a good feeler he was.

Then we turned back to the ape enclosure and there he spotted it, and he now had the wherewithal to recognise an ape visually. And after a while he no longer needed to correlate with touch in this sort of way: an autonomous visual world started to emerge – he started to find salience and meaning and to recognise things. It was almost as if some wonderful spontaneous business of selection was occurring – selection of what was important and important for him."

Dr Oliver Sachs - Quoted in Horizon – 24th January 1994

In relating this kind of evidence to the development of young children it becomes obvious that the absence of stimulation of any of the essential sensory experiences is likely to have a long-lasting detrimental effect on a balanced overall development. So if we believe in developing strong synapses as a result of continued and meaningful use, it goes without saying that some aspects of brain development must not be satisfied at the expense of others. In other words certain sensory experiences are not deemed more important than others.

As the child builds more and more synapses, increasing the synaptic density through interaction with the world, more abstract levels and cycles of action and thought become possible, every action and thought suffused with value. What this means is that even the highest levels of thinking, the most abstract kinds of human thinking are based first and fundamentally on feeling and on value. Human thought is not solely logical, it is also emotional.

**What happens now?**

How does this idea sit with the current ideas about teaching and learning and intelligence? People, who are intelligent, are often described as those who can organise their thoughts coherently, express them clearly and come to a reasoned conclusion. In school, this is frequently identified only in children who can reason verbally and mathematically. At some levels and in some education forums, this is the only identification of intelligence.

To quote my own lecture notes, in a recent example I gave to a group of teachers trying to illustrate this same point:

**"Don't ask how intelligent is David Beckham? Ask, How David Beckham is intelligent?!"**

Many of the dimensions of teaching and learning, at first sight, seem to be governed by ease of measurement whilst simultaneously some of the most creative aspects of teaching and learning almost, at times, defy measurement.

As we develop our interaction with the world around us and are stimulated by it, our thoughts, ideas and recollections of it are in visual images, we think visually. We don't think visually and then put those images to one side as inferior only to replace them with words. We think visually, aurally, spatially and kinaesthetically and in other ways too, but one way is not more intelligent than another, or better, it is different.

It is true to say that there has been an upsurge recently in teachers wanting to understand more about this way of thinking in order to further develop the quality teaching and learning. Perhaps this is a backlash from an over emphasis on the teaching styles of the core subjects of Literacy, Numeracy and Science, which for a time were taught mostly didactically even using a clock to limit sequences of teaching! Popular phrases have emerged together with catchy aide memoirs to advance novel ideas about other methods and the buzzword in some staff rooms has consequently been to use the terminology VAK (Visual, Auditory and Kinaesthetic). Unfortunately many teachers have been enthused by the principles of the importance of these elements of learning but have returned to the classroom without the skills of implementation.

I am reminded that dehydration of the brain can impair the learning process. Once acknowledged, many schools have readily provided bottled water and put up with the inconvenience of more frequent visits to the toilet! If only the development of a Creative Curriculum with VAK as one of its many dimensions could be resolved as easily as this! To make proper use of VAK principles we must return again to our understanding of how the brain develops.

Everything seems to be hinged on the transmitting and receptor neurons and the synapse (joining up) which takes place between them. We are now certain that different neurons in different parts of the brain await stimulation, which comes chiefly through sensory interaction with the world around us – our experience.

**It is also important to remember that neurons which are rigorously stimulated become stronger and those which are not used and stimulated are pruned, never to be available ever again.**

Rich experiences are stimulating and the brain also needs a stable and predictably consistent environment to flourish - what then happens to the experience is of course critical.

As stated earlier, Christian Schiller reminds us that experience is "not like a flash photograph". Frequently in the early stages of learning, the learner needs to be trained in ways that enable them to hold on to experience and then have some meaningful way of interpreting that experience.

Holding on to experience and subsequently making the most of it is essential if the brain is going to be stimulated in the best way. Learning to look, learning to see and then realising what you have or have not seen is the critical path which all learners have to encounter. Whilst there is danger in being over prescriptive in recommendations as to how to ensure that the best opportunities are created, there is also simultaneously a danger that, left to their own devices, children can pass by a wealth of opportunities because they are either not trained to look closely or are readily distracted. Even an actor must depend not only on his memory of emotions, but also on his keenness of observation. An actor friend of mine has intentionally developed a keenness of observation that he can draw upon at any time, for example how someone blows their nose. He says that he has watched, almost subconsciously, many, many ways that different people do this so that now if he is portraying a character who this behaviour fits, he can re-enact the exact movements and gestures.

I once followed a group of children around Lincoln Cathedral: they had been given work sheets to fill in. As they rushed from one 'seen-it' to another, there was nothing that held their attention. All that was required was that they tick all the boxes on their sheet before it was time for lunch. By the time they had finished, they had looked at everything and seen nothing. This kind of surface learning leaves the brain as quickly as it enters – there is little chance for neurons to build the complex connection that a Cathedral visit would offer. Deep learning which will stimulate the neurons in a way which causes other connections to be made only comes about if the learner can be 'held' longer in the presence of the looking. Good teaching finds specific ways in order to ensure that this will happen naturally.

All of us need to take information and imbed it in experiences as part of the learning process, so that it comes together for us as a meaningful event, lasting forever.

The brain is capable of learning all the time. This means that we continuously learn from all our experiences throughout our entire lives. From the vantage point of the brain 'we become what we experience'.

Robert Ornstein and others tell us that "**there are more connections possible in one human brain... connections representing feeling, emotions, thoughts... than there are atoms in the universe".** It means that our learning, our capacity to understand, our capacity to experience is virtually unlimited. It is obvious that it is through this kind of potential that creativity will flourish, making connections is of the utmost importance. At the synapse the neuro-transmitters will best function through secure connections made every day in the classroom environment where learning is embedded in worthwhile and relevant experiences

This extract from a School Council publication is still as valid today as when it was first printed and lucidly draws together many of these principles.

"The undeniable quality of education which exists in certain schools, stems in great measure from the teacher's appreciation of the nature of the child, from a sensitive understanding of the child's view of the world and from endeavours to create a school environment, which encourages learning through the child's relationship with the world.

It is a unique relationship. The child has an intensely personal delight in experiencing things, regarded by many adults as being of little interest or importance. Watch a young child playing in a rain-filled gutter, looking in a pond, studying a grasshopper or dissecting a plant, and the involvement, discipline and dedication are clear.

In a sympathetic environment children will often be deeply involved with objects adults may take for granted – a gnarled piece of wood, a mossy stone, an earthworm or perhaps a snail. We should be conscious of the scale of the child's world – often of most importance to the child is what is possible for him or her to hold in a cupped hand.

Teachers who are sensitive to this characteristic relationship between the child and his or her world, seek to create a classroom environment where rocks and shells, creatures and bones, grasses and earth are considered, together with the vast range of man-made things which surround and fascinate the child, as fundamental resources for learning in school. The introduction of such materials comes from an understanding of children, the scale of their world and their manner of involvement in it.

The basis of children's understanding of themselves and their environment is formed through information accumulated through sensory experience.

The child is full of a sensory appreciation which seems to lose its keen edge as we grow. To the child, the world offers abundant interest, sight and sound, smells and textures which help to form the fund of knowledge, which is the foundation for other learning. Experiences are fresh and untainted by adult preconditioned responses."

### Summary of principles of brain-based teaching and learning

1.  Each healthy human brain, irrespective of age, sex, nationality or cultural background, comes equipped with a set of exceptional features. These include: the ability to detect patterns and make approximations; a phenomenal capacity for various types of memory; the ability to self-correct and learn from experience by the analysis of external data and self-reflection; and an inexhaustible capacity to be creative.

2.  The brain is a parallel processor. Thoughts, intuitions, pre-dispositions and emotions operate simultaneously and interact with other modes of information. Good teaching takes this into consideration. That is why we talk about the teacher as an orchestrator of learning.

3.  Learning engages the entire physiology. The physical health of the child – the amount of sleep, the nutrition – affects the brain. The brain must be nourished and tired brains do not work at their best. Fatigue affects the brain's memory.

## The search for meaning

Children are naturally programmed to search for meaning. This principle is survival orientated. The brain needs and automatically registers the familiar, while simultaneously searching for and responding to additional stimuli. Consequently the learning environment needs to provide familiarity, frameworks, stability and security – but provision must also be made to satisfy the hunger for novelty, discovery and challenge.

Children naturally search for meaning in their lives which means that the teacher must allow for children to have rich experiences and then give them time and opportunities to make sense of their experiences. They have to have a chance to reflect, to see how things relate. One of the richest sources of learning from the point of view of the brain is the learning that is available to us through experiences. It therefore follows that the kind of learning experiences we give children shape the brains potential..

The search for meaning occurs through 'patterning' and patterning refers to the organisation and categorisation of information. The brain resists having meaningless patterns imposed upon it. By 'meaningless', I mean isolated and unrelated pieces of information. When the brain's natural capacity to integrate information is evoked in teaching, vast amounts of seemingly unrelated or random information and activities can be presented and assimilated. The brain tries to make sense of the information by reducing this to familiar patterns, if it can't it rejects it, forgets it.

Patterning is everywhere. We want to impose our patterns on what we see, and breaking patterns is very difficult. During the first few years of their lives children are as an "open system", taking in information and experiences and drawing conclusions. For the rest of their lives they go around proving that what they concluded is in fact true.

The ideal process in learning is to present information in a way that allows the brain to extract patterns rather than have them imposed and this has huge implications for teaching method. The brain is capable of taking in enormous amounts of information when that information is related in a way so that the brain can pattern it appropriately.

The ideas behind thematic teaching and an integrated curriculum are based on this principle of looking for relationships and seeing interrelated patterns. Through themes all kinds of different ideas can be related. When we consciously do this through curricular planning, the brain tends to remember many more things. Patterning is the reason.

Emotion is also critical to embedding patterning. Emotion cannot be separated out from cognition. Everything has some emotion to it. In fact, many brain researchers now believe that there is no memory without emotion. Emotions are what motivates us to learn, and more importantly to create. They are in our moods, our passion, they are a part of who we are as human beings.

### Children learn from everything.

Everything goes into the brain. As I have said, in the early years children literally become their experiences. Therefore, the environment is very important and if they learn something in the classroom and never use it outside the classroom, then that learning, those connections, stop there. In some societies, children are continually immersed in learning in the school, in the home and in the community. Their learning is seamless is used and expanded upon, they interact with each other and build experience all the time. This makes the kind of learning which is provided for less fortunate children, the child who is the product of a dysfunctional family, all the more critical in helping to provide a balanced learning opportunity. It is said that we all learn much more than we ever consciously understand. Most of the signals that are peripherally perceived enter the brain without our awareness and interact on unconscious levels. That is why learners become their experience and remember what they experience, not just what they are told.

What we call 'active processing' allows children to review how and what they have absorbed, so they begin to take charge of their learning and of the development of personal meaning. Meaning is not always evident and often happens intuitively in ways that we do not understand. So frequently, when we learn, we use both conscious and unconscious processes to acquire our understanding. The brain understands and remembers best when facts and skills are embedded in natural spatial memory so the best learning takes place by immersing learners in well-orchestrated life-like, low-threat and highly challenging learning experiences. In this way, learning comes alive in the minds of learners, so helping them to make connections in the brain which become their being.

# CHAPTER 4: MAKING IT HAPPENIN SCHOOLS

# CHAPTER**4**: **Making It Happen In Schools**

## PRE-REQUISITES

It should now be evident that I believe that for Creativity to thrive rather than survive there are certain prerequisites for the teacher, the teacher's classroom, in fact the whole school. My assumption is that as an ideal a child begins their education at Nursery level and stays in that same school until the end of Key Stage 2. My reason for needing to set this as the model is that I strongly believe in planned progression in Primary education week on week, term on term, year on year and this is best achieved in a curriculum management which acknowledges that need for continuity.

A number of years ago I was fortunate to be working in a school with a group, a small group of Year one children. It was autumn and the teacher had planned for the children to work on autumn fruits and vegetables. I chose to focus with my small group, on how they were recording all their observations about a sweetcorn. They were drawing but needed guidance on how to focus their looking more closely in order that the kind of marks they made to describe their sweetcorn were more carefully considered. We talked, stroked, smelt and considered the sweetcorn in as many ways as possible – the time came to start drawing. Most of the children were in the habit of taking about three minutes on such an activity – I explained that it would probably take all morning! It did. With my encouragement, it carried over, for some children into the afternoon and for one child whose attention to the task was total – to the next day.

*Child - Year 2*

I have revisited the school in subsequent years to remind myself and the teachers how hard they needed to work to ensure that this child was able to build on that achievement in subsequent years, term by term, year by year. In Year 6 - her final year - her drawing developed to high levels of achievement because of planned progress. All those years ago she found something she could do, the more she did it the better she became. Now given the opportunity to work in this way, she is in her element and has found a medium best suited for her to describe her experiences. She is a highly creative child who has found her medium and developed a level of skills to control it. She has been surrounded in school by stimulating and challenging experiences, which complement the kinds of experiences her parents give her at home. We could say she is fortunate. I prefer to believe that the kind of education she has received is her birthright, but what an achievement that the school enabled her to reach her true potential.

*Same Child - Year 5*

So to return to the central question of the book, "Creativity – how do we enable it to happen"? I have focussed on the importance of Experience and identified the differences in schemata. I now want to focus on other characteristics which are essential for creativity to flourish.

## Observation

**"As we increase the range of what we see, we increase the richness of what we can imagine"**

Ruskin

In his book *The Creative Imagination* Kenneth Barnes writes:

'To observe – to take notice of – is in some measure to experience, and observation therefore implies experience. No knowledge is possible without an act of synthesis on the part of the knower, some kind of putting together, the imagining of a relationship. There can be no such thing as "mere" observation, a passive mind receiving an imprint. We bring something of ourselves to the discrimination of the most trivial object in the outside world.'

Observation is, however, interpreted in different ways as I have already suggested earlier and I want to emphasise here how important it is in relation to experience. Without observation, experience can simply pass us by. I believe that observational skills should be the foundation of all meaningful learning. It stimulates thought by building a repertoire of images and understanding which in turn increases learning potential and intensifies the characteristics of learning development. Writers, musicians, scientists, all must observe nature and humanity in order to shape their knowledge. The more sensitive their perception is, the more likely they are to be able to be innovative and original in their achievement, ie to be creative

How frequently we hear of scientists finding similarities or differences between say, for example, plants or animals. This is frequently only achieved by close and detailed observation; the kind of observation which an artist would engage in if drawing or painting.

**"What is seen depends on how the observer allocates his attention, i.e. on the anticipation he develops and the perceptual explorations he carries out"**

Ulric Noisser – Cognition and Reality

Noisser rightly draws our attention to 'how'. Observation is no aimless relaxation, it is an active, outward-going focus of attention. Observation focuses on the essential characteristics which differentiate one thing from another and recognises patterns and similarities. So at different stages of development and with different stimuli, the teacher gradually develops the skills of observing. Only highly skilled observers with years of experience can assimilate a large number of aspects of a subject and consequently the good teacher will break down that number to focus on one aspect of a subject – for example, the texture of the material from which it is made. So, with guidance, the child selects certain aspects of a subject and in so doing relates what is seen to what is already known or imagined. Sometimes this is done subconsciously, sometimes through questioning and sometimes with help from the teacher. In this way we build our schemata.

**"I personally think that it's a question of curiosity, wanting to explain things, having a love of phenomena. I think just to look at a rainbow or the stamen of a flower and wondering what it does, why it's there, what produces it and our reaction to it is really what science is all about. Initially it's a response to nature and the thing to do, I think, first of all is simply to look at let's say a butterfly emerging, a marvellous thing to see it coming from its pupa, wings**

drying out and becoming a different live form, that sort of thing. I can actually remember when I was at kindergarten seeing that, we got this big pupa, put it in a little box, we made it, we watched this thing coming out. I've never forgotten it and to my mind that sort of lesson is both an intensely emotional experience, you really feel the wonder of nature, then later on you think about the mechanism, how do the wings grow and that evokes the imagination, stimulates the imagination in a sort of creative way".

Richard Gregory

With all the distractions which surround children at home and even in schools, focussed and concentrated observation is difficult. Behaviour patterns and expectations have to be clearly defined so that all our children dispose themselves in a manner which shows that they are striving to be engaged and not distracted. It is during these intense moments which, even with young children, focus of attention can be extended to quite long periods of time. Then the child begins to 'live' within the experience of looking - personal memories and associations come to mind which can arouse emotions and intense feelings. Later these experiences can, in turn, lead on to imagining. Where children are encouraged to develop their learning in this way, they frequently find incredible fulfilment.

*Child - Year 5*

As we grow older, certainly almost as soon as children leave their Primary School, associative vision, the immediate identification and association of an object with a conditional response to it, becomes a norm in behaviour.

I was once taking a group of children around Lincoln Cathedral. As we slowly walked up the aisle I was pointing out various aspects of the building, which I thought might be the starting point for further work. As we approached the nave, the organ started to play - I asked the children to stop and listen. As we were about to move on, the small girl standing next to me questioned, "Alright mister we've seen the cathedral and heard the music, when are we going to do something cool...?" We had been in the building only fifteen minutes. It is up to the adult, parent or teacher to capture the moment of curiosity early and provide the child from the very earliest beginnings with skills of engagement in observation. Factual observation is only concerned with picking up the essential information needed at a particular moment. "What time is it?", is a question which focuses the attention on the time, not on the clock, its size, shape, colour, roman numerals or whether it had a second hand. If however children are alert and keen observers, they will collect all that information and more, which in turn will nourish and enhance their creative potential.

As William Walsh writes in The Use of Imagination:

**"'An image is more than a representation of an object: in it lurks dim meanings and indistinct connections which together form mental patterns long before the child can elaborate them rationally",**

And, as Marie Clay reminds us:

**"We must always remember that his eye may perceive more than his hand can execute, more than his tongue can tell"**

When it comes to the point of using observations in story writing, scientific hypothesis, poetry, painting or perhaps dance, the child selects from what has been seen or felt or even imagined and confidently reassembles these, expressing his ideas through symbols. In this way the visual and sensory experience is formalised. So in time the more the child looks and has time to contemplate what he/she sees, the richer and more personal will be the symbolism and the greater the confidence in recording ideas.

**To look at anything**

**If you would know that thing**

**You must look at it long**

**To look at this green and say**

**I have seen Spring in these woods, will not do, you must be the dark snake of stems and ferny plumes**

**You must enter into the small silences between the leaves**

**You must take your time and touch the very peace they issue from**

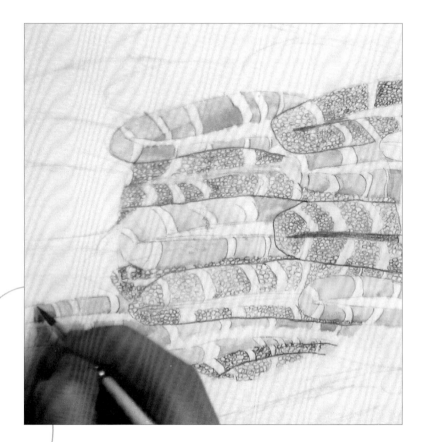

# TAKING RISKS

### "Being creative is a leap into the dark"

Picasso

This implies taking risks, experimenting and making mistakes. In order that creativity can flourish there must be a balance between the response to the stimulus and the skills needed to interpret it. Earlier, I instanced my own early experience with woodwork, concentrating on the skill with little or no concern for application, let alone imagination. In contrast, too much stimulus can be equally problematical.

**I was working in a school which was gradually developing the kind of principles which this book is promoting. The school was midway through a review of its curriculum and wanting to enrich the children's experiences in school. It had been decided to invite a steel band from another school to demonstrate their undoubted skills to children in Years Five and Six – about a hundred children in all.**

**In their classrooms, the children were well behaved with only the occasional need for behaviour to be modified, nothing that could not be easily corrected by teacher intervention. Gathered together in a large number, their class teachers in attendance plus the headteacher and the visiting teachers who managed the children in the steel band, they were excited by the atmosphere, the music and the group dynamics. Who it was who first began to sway to the music, I cannot say. The sway became a swing, the swing a jive, the jive a rave and suddenly there was chaos! Those who chose not to dance saw it as an opportunity to climb the wall bars, aggression quickly emerged as children collided and just in time, in fear of our lives and theirs,**

I return to the children working on the clay model of the otter. These photographs capture moments of individual reflection, group debate, focussed application and sheer delight. What they do not show are the moments of fear, anticipation and frustration as bits of clay fell off when least expected, the remodelling of a foot because the first attempt was too small, the elation at finding a way to texture the surface of the clay to represent the otter's back.

These children took risks, experimented and invented things to do with clay that they had never dreamt of. The more successful they were the more they wanted to do and as they became more skilful, they reworked areas which previously had pleased them. Breaks and lunchtimes merged into a self-propelled schedule to complete the work to the very highest level.

More importantly from the teacher's point of view and the argument put forward by this text, these children had never used clay before!

The freedom of expression, which was so necessary for their work to succeed, was secured by their being taught by me and they themselves teaching each other the technical skills needed to be successful. The medium of clay was new to them but chosen because it best suited their likely need to interpret the stimulus – the otter – which none of them had seen in real life outside school. Within the scope of their achievement the children exceeded the targets which they set themselves and in the final analysis, admired four different interpretations of the one stimulus, knowing their own success - the kind of learning that stays with you for ever.

"Have a go", is a phrase which is often used to encourage children to try something, perhaps for the first time. Freedom to experiment involves taking risks. In so doing, we as adults even 'run the risk' of making mistakes or of 'looking foolish'. But 'chancing your arm', 'having a go', need not end up in disaster. Risking an intelligent guess in response to a question from a teacher is largely determined by teacher judgement in the level of questioning. We know that in order to develop intelligent thinking, teachers must create a supportive atmosphere in which children are encouraged and prepared to 'have a go'. If they don't, the child will quickly learn to play safe which has the effect of dumbing-down the whole teaching and learning potential.

Children who are prepared to engage seriously in learning in this way are likely to have one of the critical attributes of being highly creative. Creative learners are not committed to the preservation of the status quo, they are more likely to be flexible and adaptable and prepared to change their mind and opinion in the light of their experience and the experiences of their peers.

There is clearly a direct link between learning a skill and playing with and exploring a medium or material. Too much time learning routines practised every day in a dull and unenlightened way can develop a bored and frustrated child and as I have already intimated, too much freedom can lead to chaos. Creativity carries within it the idea of action and purpose, the freedom to change and modify as seems best in the moment or later on reflection.

Twenty years ago I read an article in the 'Listener', where Richard Feynman described his work on the quantum theory at Cornell University with Hans Bethe:

## My father taught me to notice things

One day I was playing with an express wagon, a little wagon which has a railing around it for children to play with. It had a ball in it. I pulled the wagon and I noticed something about the way the ball moved. I went to my father and said: 'Say, Pop, I noticed something. When I pull the wagon the ball rolls to the front of the wagon. Why is that?" And he said: 'Nobody knows. The general principle is that things that are moving try to keep on moving, and things that are standing still tend to stand still unless you push them hard. This tendency is called "inertia", but nobody knows why it's true.'

Now that showed a deep understanding. He didn't give me a name. He knew the difference between knowing the name of something and knowing something, which I learnt very early. He went on to say: 'If you look close you'll find the ball does not rush to the back of the wagon. It's the back of the wagon that you're pulling towards the ball. The ball stands still, or, as a matter of fact, from the friction, starts to move forward, really. It doesn't move back.

So I ran back and set the ball up again and pulled the wagon from under it. I looked sideways and saw that indeed he was right. The ball never moved backwards in the wagon when I pulled the wagon forward. It moved forward a little bit, and the wagon caught up with it. So that's the way I was educated by my father, with that kind of example. No pressure, just lovely, interesting discussions.

One day I thought to myself: I haven't done anything important, and I'm never going to do anything important. But I used to enjoy physics and mathematical things. It was never very important, but I used to do things for the fun of it. So I decided: I'm going to do things only for the fun of it.

That afternoon, while I was eating lunch, some kid threw a plate in the cafeteria. There was a blue medallion on the plate, the Cornell sign. He threw the plate up, and as it came down it spun and it wobbled, and I wondered what the relation was between the two. I was just playing; it had no importance at all. So I played around with the equations of motion of rotating things and I found out that if the wobble was small, the blue thing went round twice as fast as the wobble went round. Then I tried to figure out why that was, directly from Newton's laws instead of through the complicated equations, and I worked that out for the fun of it.

Then I went to Hans Bethe and said: 'Hey, I'll show you something amusing.' I explained it to him and he said: 'Yes, it's very amusing and interesting, but what's the use of it?' I said: 'That doesn't make any difference. It hasn't any use. I'm just doing it for the fun of it.'

**I continued to play with this rotation and it led me to a similar problem of the rotation of the spin of an electron according to Dirac's equation, and that led me back into quantum electrodynamics, which is the problem I'd been working on. I continued playing with it in the relaxed fashion I had originally done, and it was just like taking the cork out of a bottle – everything just poured out. In very short order I worked out the things for which I later won the Nobel Prize.**

**I don't like honours. I won't have anything to do with the Nobel Prize. I'd already got the prize – the prize is the pleasure of finding the thing out, the kick in the discovery, the observation, that other people use it. Those are the real things.**

Extract from Horizon (BBC2) November 1981

Reproduced from 'The Listener' 26th November 1981

I was subsequently able to record his ideas about teaching Science for a Teacher training interactive video I was making. We discussed imagination and how imagination was perhaps different for the scientist. He replied: "In the case of Science, I think that one of the things that make it very difficult is that it takes a lot of imagination. It is very hard to imagine all the crazy things that the world is really like. Now that's kind of a lot of fun to think about. I don't want to take this stuff seriously, I think we should just have fun imagining it and not worry about it. There is no teacher going to ask you questions at the end, otherwise it's a horrible subject. You ask me if an ordinary person, by studying hard, would get to be able to imagine these things like I imagine them, of course".

At the time few teachers seemed to understand how important the links were between creative thinking and great science. When I shared many of Feynman's other learning principles with teachers on different courses, few seemed to understand why I was so enthusiastic about the insights Feynman had provided. As probably one of the most original thinkers of the 20th century, he had described so clearly how the best scientists are, in fact, very imaginative, have fun, take risks and don't worry about 'having a go'.

You can imagine my surprise and delight when nearly twenty years later, with the publication of 'All our futures' by the DfEE, a synopsis of the article from all those years ago appeared on page 29. Perhaps all the heart searching had not been in vain.

I want to draw this section to a conclusion by explaining how I come to have such particular beliefs and ideals.

## Looking Back

**"It is only when I look back that
I can anticipate the future"**

Mark Twain

**Coming to the end of my secondary school career, I was lucky enough to win a scholarship to work in the Picasso potteries in Vallaurice in Southern France. At that stage in my life I left a very sheltered upbringing in a small market town in Lincolnshire, I had never been away on holiday on my own and never left the United Kingdom.**

**I arrived in Southern France to experience a climate and way of life that was completely new with a very basic knowledge of the language. I had no idea what I had let myself in for – I just arrived. It took all of twelve hours for me to realise that a working scholarship was what it was and at five o'clock on the first morning I joined four men and walked the mile and a half to the clay pits. We began the**

daily duty of digging, transporting and wedging the clay for the studio workshops. Until that morning I had never handled clay throughout my entire education in school and had only encountered it on my father's allotment, where it was regarded by him, as a confounded nuisance. Chopping it out of the pit was a formidable task – it was unyielding to my digging and levering. As the others filled their huge panniers, they laughed at my inexperienced and totally ineffectual attempts to fill half a pannier. As I recollect, they left me with the feeling of total inadequacy for two or three days and then one morning, elbowing me out of my muddle, Marc, a man of about forty, showed me how to dig. I tried, failed, tried gain and with close encouragement, suddenly I could do it. They all cheered as I filled my pannier with comparative ease – I had become apprenticed to Marc, an expert in clay. A very significant day in my life.

The long walk back with the clay was effort enough but on arrival at the studios, the real work began, breaking down the huge blocks to fist size pieces and feeding them into a crusher – what I now know to be a pug mill.

Having pulverised and compacted the clay, it was extruded from the machine in huge coiled lengths which were then barrowed to a waiting standpit. Here water was thrown over the entire heap which was shielded from the full heat of the sun by raffia screens and damp sacking. The clay remained in these heaps until it was covered with a green slime – this took three to four weeks – then it was ready to be worked. The studio yard had several hundred standpits, each new day a new one was chosen which was 'ripe' – the nearest translation of the French.

It was here that my second apprenticeship began which took

all of two weeks. I had to learn how to wedge clay until it was exactly the right consistency for the potter's wheel. The craftsmen who surrounded me could wedge clay and talk and joke at the same time. I had to focus my attention totally, practising the routine until it became second nature. The objective – I had to know almost instinctively when the clay was right. If anyone has ever written a book to describe this condition, I have never seen it, but after about three weeks I could get it right every time.

When I left home I had perhaps imagined on my train journey across France that I would be making beautiful ceramic forms – not so, but the best was still to come.

We have all watched the potter at the wheel and today, with powered electric wheels, much of the rhythm and oneness with the materials and the process of the skill has disappeared. In the early stages of becoming a potter at the wheel, there are many similarities with learning to ride a bicycle. With one foot supporting my own weight I had to keep the huge stone drive wheel at a constant speed, know how and when to slow it and more importantly, stop it. The consequences of not being able to manage these simple skills were as disastrous as mistakes in cycling.

So I knew the clay and gradually mastered the propelling skill of the wheel, then came the time to put it all together. If the clay is too hard or too soft, the task is impossible. If the speed of the wheel is too fast or too slow, the clay either skids away or remains in an ungainly lump.

The potter is intent on centring the clay and to do this he must know himself, his limitations, know his material and how to control it and lastly, take risks with it in order to form it into the shape he intends.

I believe this word 'centring' and its action has much to teach us about being a learner. Remaining calm, motivated and focussed, the learner takes the material or medium and knowing it, can shape and mould it. Being at one with the material, in your element, releases the creative potential and the opportunity to experiment, push boundaries to the limit and take risks.

But to complete the explanation;

**Too much clay on the wheel head is a battle of strength. Too little and there is not enough to contain and control; but as the wheel spins by applying pressure with the heel of the hand, the clay centres itself. By squeezing it, the clay rises and with a downward pressure from the palm it returns to a central conical form, time and time again. This is rehearsed until it is as the rhythm in a dance.**

**The potter now comes to the most difficult part of all, to translate the form that is in his head, through his hands into the clay. Hollow cylindrical forms are the simplest, but of course, the risks are greater and greater the further the shape moves away from this logical structure. Plastic and spinning at high speed, what other shape could there possibly be?**

**Experience now comes into play and gradually a balance is achieved between taking risks and controlling the medium. In potting, it is disastrous to ignore that balance and those who do so are left with a heap of wet mud when the intention of the activity was to create a beautiful form.**

The potter's success is also determined by reorganizing the distinction between focal and subsidiary awareness, both of which, as I have described, are very important. As I kick the weighted wheel around, if I become distracted from the critical relationship of my hands drawing up the moving cylinder of clay, and think about why my leg is tired, disaster will follow and I will lose the form I am creating.

My focus is the clay and subsidarily I am aware of my foot kicking the wheel, maintaining the speed. In this case and generally, subsidiary and focal awareness are mutually exclusive. Without maintaining the speed of the wheel the clay will not rise. Without my hands being exactly opposite each other as I apply pressure to the clay, the clay will not be shaped. The problems of my granddaughter in learning to ride a bicycle, referred to in a previous chapter, can now be seen to have parallels with the potter, as also with the dancer and the painter and the musician.

Lastly, it is important to emphasise again that as the clay is worked on the wheel, so the material itself, if the potter has mastered the medium, can suggest new forms and possibilities, sometimes even born out of error. Creativity in this example is a dialogue between concept and material and as such, is no different in the development of music, dance, painting, poetry or scientific and technological invention. Clay will always for me, remain a unique experience for the rest of my life. After all, **'we become what we repeatedly do'.**

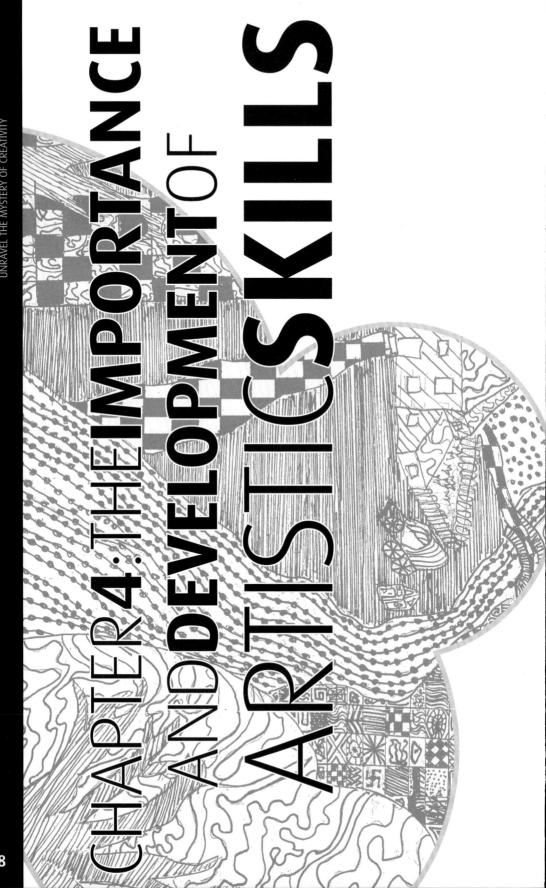

# CHAPTER 4: THE IMPORTANCE AND DEVELOPMENT OF ARTISTIC SKILLS

# CHAPTER4: **The Importance and Development of Artistic Skills**

Generally speaking artistic development involves the education of the making, perceiving and feeling systems.

**"Every genuinely creative worker must gain in one way or another, such a full understanding of his medium and such skill, ingenuity and flexibility in handling it, that he can make fresh use of it to create anew."**

Ghiselin. B. The Creative Process. Mentor 1961. p29

## What Skills?

How children, indeed artists in any creative sphere, acquire control of their medium and have command over it is one of the most important aspects of creative / aesthetic education. Teachers know that through constant practice with a medium and continuing exploration of it, confidences develop which enable the creation of new symbols to express ideas.

In the classroom, in any learning for that matter, the practice of skills will not be successfully developed by coercion. Motivation must, at least in the initial stages, come from within so the immersion in the process can be said and often seen to be self-motivated. Certainly, in early childhood, there is a delight in the spontaneity - that unfettered making and doing activity. What the teacher must be careful to avoid is crushing the spontaneity in order to teach the skill!

Children are fascinated with words and will invent their own, they will sing and explore noises in their throats and mouths. In music, they will willingly explore the potential of instruments, in painting, the rich variety of colour. All these explorations are essential stages in the development of skills. But skills are not naturally acquired just through exploration of a medium and it may be that one of the reasons that the visual and performing arts deteriorated from having an important part to play in education, was because there often seemed to be little understanding of the need to teach skills and plan for their gradual and rehearsed development.

So the teacher is continually faced with the problem or opportunity of the choice between explicit instruction or direction, creating a situation where the skill is likely to develop. We can liken this latter idea to the role of the apprentice who, working alongside a skilled creator, gradually learns the first rudimentary practises, then is allowed to take-on more difficult tasks until, through a combination of emulation and experimentation within boundaries, a skill is acquired.

**For example, I recently watched a group of children, about thirty in all, practising marching. Some could, others couldn't. In fact the variation of skill between the group was unbelievable. They had as their model, a sergeant major whose patience was tested to the limit, but he was tolerant, patient and kind. The early steps were slow and measured, some tried watching others, some tried watching their own feet, repeating left, right, left, right but not being able to relate their words to their foot movements.**

I visited the same children with their trainer three weeks later and applauded their progress. Their coordination had improved and to a person, they marched to the rhythm of a drum. I commended them. Their trainer turned to me smiling. "The best is yet to come – you see we can only march in a straight line at the moment, we are now going to learn how to turn through a right angle!!"

The importance of having someone breaking down the stages of skill development into what we call "bite-sized chunks", is so important but at the same time the child needs to have a clear idea of what is possible, where they are heading.

The children I met were anticipating a visit to see a full parade of marching soldiers. Through the visit the children might appreciate their skills and realise what they might achieve if they continued to practice their own marching skills.

Imitation and replication, are important aspects of creative development. The child cannot know what is possible with a medium by only being allowed to copy what others have done before. This could deter any creative potential and at worst, set objectives which are too high and seemingly beyond reach.

Imitation, copying and replicating adult achievement is critical in creative development, yet paradoxically can limit a child's creative potential by apparently setting unattainable goals.

I visited a class of six and seven year olds who were learning about painting in the style of Monet. Each child had a coloured postcard of the 'Lily Pond' and was attempting to copy it onto large sheets of paper, using large brushes and ready mixed paint. When I later talked to the class, none had ever seen a lily pond and were incredulous that the painting they had been copying from a postcard, which still hangs in Monet's studio where he had painted it, was bigger than one wall of their classroom.

This was an example of a total misunderstanding of how skills and inappropriate unattainable goals can destroy creative potential.

**Children need to:**

1) Explore the medium as freely as possible

2) Learn sufficient skills to gain mastery of the medium to realise its potential.

3) Hold an image in their minds which represents their own ideas about a subject.

I referred earlier to a period in the past when there seemed little understanding about the development of artistic skills, both in the visual and performing arts. In truth, there is a hierarchy of skills in all the creative arts which can and should be planned for and clearly set out with defined objectives.

One of the activities which I believe has undermined the principles and practices this book seeks to advocate has been the use of screwed-up tissue paper as a creative medium! No-one who has done this activity needs to do it again to become better at it and yet, I have seen children as old as eight years aimlessly messing about with it in the name of creativity and the product of their efforts showing no more than that it was a worthless time-filling activity.

## Achieving Mastery

It must be evident that every art form requires certain technical skills. Many examples can be listed but in order to clarify the point, let us consider mixing paint.

It could be said from the outset that this is no discussion point since paint can be purchased and given to children 'ready-mixed' in every primary, secondary and tertiary colour. This avoids, for example, having to choose from a range of reds, blues, and yellows, black or white. This denies children the opportunity to learn to select the appropriate colours to mix, to be able to discriminate one tone from another, to match the colour mixed on the brush with the intended choice of colour to interpret the subject, all are advanced painting skills. The application of that paint, its luminosity or density, transparency or texture add yet further decisions to developing a complex skill base.

These kinds of skills are of course very different but of equal importance to the skills of the dancer, whose physical expression or interpretation is dependent entirely on the acquisition of high levels of motor dexterity and muscular control. In order to express ideas, the dancer has to build confidence in being able to put together a sequence of skills in such a way that the expression itself appears effortless. So just as the painter mixes green many times in order to know how to call upon that experience to represent a specific subject, so too the dancer learns particular rote sequences 'by heart' in order to freely bring them together to interpret a gesture.

Repeating an activity which has become an acquired skill is of great satisfaction to the child - the good teacher encourages this. "See if you can feel that again – relive it". This in turn helps to raise confidence and self-esteem as it is achieved and of course, establishes even stronger patterns and pathways of experience in the brain. There is also no doubt that acquiring a skill is hard and arduous work for the child. Some of it exists outside the comfort zone but in aquiring the skill, the accomplishment, the pride and self-esteem are rewards in their own right. There is no easy route to the mastery of a skill but it can certainly be made easier by encouragement and support. Realising that you cannot do something very well may inform your reasoning that you are not very good at it, but a skilled teacher can and will turn that lack of success around through positive reinforcement - working alongside the child as in the apprenticeship model, or by finding an alternative approach.

It is here of course that the teacher can come into their own and perhaps strangely, in this context, I instance a group of children with whom I was asked to work with recently to develop their writing. As with many others of a similar age, 6 years, their writing failed to develop beyond what can only be described as a 'flat, monosyllabic drone'. On examination of what was taking place, their work lacked any feeling or substance. They did have a number of skills however, many of them could write in sentences, use capital letters and full stops and give an example, when asked, of an adjective - surprisingly, their work contained very few adjectives. What was missing for many was simply stimulation, something to write about – that moved them to want to find adjectives to describe the quality of their experiences. The reason they were not succeeding was because they had nothing to say!!

A lack of strong feeling and suggestive experiences can thwart the creative spirit and frequently children can respond to a simple suggestion which seems to unlock a totally different approach to learning. "Last night I dreamt that...". "Once I used to... but now". "You are that bird perched on a cliff, how does it feel"? "Write a poem with a lie in every line". This is no challenge to the orthodoxy of the Literacy Strategy but a suggestion that once the framework becomes a matter of course, children, with the teacher's approval, need to take risks and experiment with the skills of their own language, their own ideas and experiences.

The most important aspect of our understanding of the creative process brings us back to the intensity of the experience and its interpretation through the chosen symbolic medium.

A group of seven year olds wrote some of the most evocative writing I have read for that age, about the Fire of London. Being a long way from London and having no experience of fire, they built models of a London street typical of the time, from cardboard, wood and straw. Overnight, the class teacher, a young man at the beginning of his teaching career, set fire to them! On arrival at school the next morning the children expressed all the emotions that the real experience would have engendered. An extreme example but the quality of the writing justified method.

**Excitement in the air**

There it was, the gannet gliding gently to a ledge, softly landing, grass thinly covers the tiny ledge. Other birds soar the unspoiled sky. Fluffy white clouds dot the pale blue sky. Shadows lurk on the deep blue sea. A lonely kittiwake cries its shrill cry. The puffin sits comfortably on his tiny, narrow ledge. A tern glides swiftly across the ocean waves. The foaming, roaring sea crashes against the rocks. A group of clever guillemots dive and quickly scoop up a small. A yellow head silently glides by the telescope. I carefully moved to the wire and peeped over. There not there metres away was a puffin its coloured beak in full view. Its glossy black feathers seem to shine like a furnace. A black headed gull swoop across the blue sea. The white foam clashes with with the chalky rock.

A gannet swiftly glides across the roaring sea. White foam spreads across the roaring, growling deep sea. Cries are heard above the roar of the sea, grass dots the chalky cliff. A guillemot jumps into the hungry water. Cliffs are covered with flapping wings and movement. Long grass blows in the gentle breeze. Foam chases the greedy wave. A colourful beak flashes past the end of the telescope which is green and fastened to the fence by a clamp. Razorbills fly quickly across the cliff face. Cliffs look as if they are going to slip into the sea.

Cannot fly over the foaming sea. The waves look like white horses galloping across a .blue, plain. Shadows are cast as gannets gulls and other birds fly across the deep, dark

*Child - Year 4/5.*

Life at the time of the fire of London in 1666.

BY DANIEL GROVE.

Before the fire there was a terrible plague it killed more than 1000 people so a dof came to each house a q wackdoctor people called them because they wore a mask like a duck's beak so the doctor would not catch there germs, that the person he had came to and the beak would smell of herbs and he called something like a large pin ane he would poke it into thierfire and pop the spots with the pin. They had a dried toad round there neck so they would not caten a cold.

The fire of LONDON Started in the pudding lane bakery of

*Child - Year 1/2*

Through the mastery of skills a realization develops in the child of the importance of the arts as a communication process. During that time the child develops his own enthusiasms and interests finding that some art forms lend themselves better than others to both his or her feeling and temperament. Once the possibilities of a medium have been realized, the child is then able to perceive stylistic variations – the differences between works, and having assimilated the different styles he encounters, determines the means of expression peculiarly best suited to both subject matter, stimulus, personality and aesthetic intention.

If we compare the adult and the child as they both strive in the mastery of skills, it is as if the adult has studied to develop a style, whereas children express themselves through the most accessible medium. Children's gifts control them – spontaneity - whereas the artist controls his or her gift and follows his/her instinct only after the medium has been mastered. So we can recognize these principles in conflict, what is for the artist - the development of the skill - a necessary, serious and sometimes arduous task is, for the child in the best learning environment, an experience of pure pleasure and natural delight and enthusiasm. It is instinctive. This makes it even more important that in school the selection of any medium and the time given to develop skills is critical. There must be a recognition of the developmental stages and the order in which they should be experienced, the choice given to match the need for expression to the most appropriate medium. By that I mean having total confidence that one has absolute control over hand and eye in the presentation of the interpretation of the idea and the feeling within it. There is a unique moment when the materials with which you have been struggling suddenly fit together and the ready completion of a work follows as if it has its own momentum. Of course this can only occur because of hours previously spent mastering the medium or means of expression.

Finally then we should consider the 'what' and the 'how'. In recent years in Primary education particularly, the emphasis has fallen increasingly on the 'what' rather than the 'how'. Primary teachers must give place and importance to visual, auditory and kinaesthetic learning. In order to do this, the teacher has to recognise and identify the child who may not be particularly adept in the explanation of an idea but is able to give enormous meaning and feeling to the language and the expression of it. In recognising this in any child and giving it the proper space and time to develop, we may be providing the simple creative opportunity for a future actor, scientist, inventor or writer.

## Providing a supportive framework

If learning a new skill, it is important to clearly define how a developmental framework of skills can be planned to support a creative curriculum.

In this instance I am going to concentrate on the visual and performing arts and in doing so I want it to be clearly understood that my views on creativity in science and mathematics are of equal relevance, but are not part of this explanation.

I am therefore interested in identifying skills which can be developed in their own right and then of equal importance, how they can be related to other skills. Just as I would wish to be able to break down the most complex dance routine into its fundamental steps and sequences of movement, so I would seek to do the same thing with, for example, drawing. From the simplest beginnings both of these disciplines have interdependent structures, which enable a developmental route to be planned to help both teachers and children progress through a sequence of known skill levels.

By considering one small element it is possible to then explore its potential, see how it relates to other creative skills and once rehearsed, a group of teachers can develop their own hierarchical model. It should be explained at this point that the model now outlined is not intended to be a definitive one, but rather a way of thinking about the kind of skills we should teach children and the kinds of exceptional people, teachers, we need to do it.

It is not possible to say where in
any ordering of the entire repertoire of
expressive and performing arts, mark-making
should be placed. It certainly does not come before talking and
walking but there may be children who, as they are struggling to
develop their walking and talking, are also learning how to hold
a tool, in this case a pencil, and have discovered that they can
control, if only in a limited way, the marks it makes. There must
be a sense of awe and wonder and possible disbelief the first time
this happens for the child.

"This tool which I hold and press down and move is different from
my finger in that it leaves a mark. I can do it again and again and
I am filled with wonder and delight that I have found another way
in which I can influence and change the world around me".

So it begins and from those first, perhaps chance, early marks a wealth of opportunity now awaits, but in order to gain better control to coordinate hand, brain and eye, much time, effort and anguish will follow. For every normal child, as a result of practice, the skill will develop that enables that child to make a mark with a pencil where it is intended and when.

**"The hand when it holds a tool is an instrument of discovery, thread a needle, fly a kite, play a recorder, the hand is the cutting edge of the mind, the refinement of learning is the refinement of the hand in action"**

Bronowski. Ascent of Man

Just as Literacy is scaffolded in order to build the structure of a text, so in the same way mark-making can be similarly planned so that through the repetition of the mark the essential patterns and rhythms of handwriting are rehearsed as are the variety and complexity of marks which when combined, enrich the potential of drawing. Once a child develops the fundamental skills of this process then learning takes off in its own right, children invent their own marks, use them in a variety of ways and relate them to images which they have experienced in the world around them. We should remind ourselves here that the purposes of the activity is to develop skills which operate at a variety of levels – mark-making in its own right, handwriting, drawing from observation to record and study a stimuli, and sheer inventive and imaginative drawings. By developing mark making in this way, a foundation is laid which acts as a model for other interpretive skills, all of which are based on these principles, although different in action and product.

The close affinity between music and dance is reassuring for the teacher since the structure of complex dance routines or orchestrations can be broken down into simple patterns of sound or movement beginning with regular rhythmic patterns as with mark making. In fact many of the early exercises developing mark-making skills are assisted and often enhanced by the use of tambour and percussion instruments. Relating marks to rhythm requires coordination and focus of application which is almost identical to early dance routines. The reader will recall my earlier description of marching rehearsals in the playground.

As confidence grows control over the medium progresses. In this case the pencil and paper, children and teachers rapidly realise that it is obvious that there are close links between monochromatic mark-making and colour and just as it is necessary for children to play with and explore any material they experience for the first time, paint needs to be introduced in the same way. Knowing that paint can be applied to different surfaces in different ways is one element of the skill-based teaching which is essential to this particular creative activity. As a skill it builds on the earlier experiences of mark making, which should precede it and then is developed in a similar way.

The sheer ecstatic enjoyment of placing, dabbing, daubing and washing on layers of colour is a prerequisite of the aesthetic experience of the material – controlling the medium comes next and lastly, as I have explained earlier, the realisation of its possibilities by looking at colour in the world around us and how it is interpreted differently by different artists, both living and dead.

I recall discussing a Van Gogh interior scene with a boy of about eight or nine years of age and eventually we focussed our attention on the floor tiles of the bedroom interior. The pattern of the perspective of the tiles had been distorted to increase their design characteristics in the painting. The boy turned to me and said, "I didn't think you were supposed to do that." I asked him if he liked it – he nodded and I continued – "if it was alright for Mr Van Gogh, it will be alright for you". Two days later I shared his painting with the whole class, pointing out the original way he had worked out the way to interpret the floor. He had the authority to emulate but in so doing, to make the idea his own.

It is worth remembering yet again that this activity is in response to stimuli. It bears no relationship to colouring in photocopied sheets and depends upon visual and emotional responses to experience. As with mark-making, there need be no end product which is measurable according to conventions such as photographic resemblance as in a portrait but there will be evidence of the engagement of the child with the medium, evidence of control over it, the capacity to exercise the widest range of uses with material and choices made in terms of appropriateness to purpose.

Another application of paint and
colouristhroughtheprintingprocess.
This requires some understanding of
the nature of marks and use of colour.
As with all interpretive skills there is a
precision which can be achieved in printing,
which is equal to the skills required when playing an
instrument with the left and right hands simultaneously. The
earliest exercises of this skill are also founded in hand, brain and
eye coordination, only in this instance the extension of the hand
is the printing block. A number of new factors become important
even in the earliest printing processes such as 'counting on', and
the mastering of that skill leads on to the potential complexities
of the skill itself. As with other skills already mentioned, the use
of music, rhythm and sequence, and the importance of dexterity
– as with movement and dance, links this interpretive discipline
very closely to other skills.

Making books with children draws together many of the skills already referred to – has strong links which are purposeful and worthwhile with the National Literacy Strategy and of course, is a design and technology activity where fit for purpose is a primary concern. As with the other identified skills, this activity has its own development route – the earliest examples created by children have a play characteristic but excite through the control and manipulation of the medium, card or paper. Fortunately each stage of development is complete in its own right and so can stand alone, but as with the other interpretive skills, the most exceptional creative work occurs once the basic skills have been mastered.

One further reason for including book-making in the control group of purposeful creative skills is the nature of authorship. For children to develop a love of Literacy, they must have insights into all aspects of authorship: the bringing together and ordering of ideas into a unified whole. The creative act of this in its own right is reason enough but it is the sense of satisfaction in the complete work – cover, page layout, illustration and overall design which provides the opportunity to bring together so many creative skills simultaneously.

Book-making brings to the creative ideal, the first opportunity to work three dimensionally even though each page is a two dimensional creation. The principle is of course radically altered with the introduction of paper engineering and pop-up pages. There is a real need in all children to make and construct three dimensionally and the sensory activities which form the central group of interpretive skills include three-dimensional work.

# Prospero's Palace

Be not afeared:
The isle is full of noises,
Sounds and sweet airs,
That give delight and hurt not.
Sometimes a thousand twangling instruments
Will hum about mine ears;
And sometimes voices,
That, if I then had waked after long sleep,
Will make me sleep again.
o~O~o

When working with fabrics, children are working in both a two and three-dimensional manner. Because fabric is pliable and resilient it lends itself well to the kind of exploration children need to go through in order to realise its true potential. Basic to the process and the cutting and fixing of fabrics, either to each other or to a background surface, a hierarchy of fixing and subsequently decorative stitching needs to be developed. Historically we have a vocabulary for different kinds of stitches which range from the most simple to highly complex. In the earliest stages these follow closely the developmental route of mark making but with fineness of control over what is, after all, a simple tool – even very young children can achieve remarkable work.

It is also worth noting that boys who have great difficulty in sustained concentration, find sewing with thread very absorbing and fulfilling. It is a skill which they can master subsequently gaining self-esteem and the potential for original creative work.

Within the central group of skill based activities is the only three dimensional material which is unique to civilization - Clay. I don't advocate that we should search out a substitute for clay any more than we should provide children with paint which you don't have to mix. There is no substitute for clay which responds uniquely to the softest stroke, the strongest squeeze or the most tearing scratch.

Once again all the time spent on the earlier skills with marks, the precision of the pressed printing block – all are brought together when working with clay. It is the only three dimensional material which responds to and reveals to the user how it has been treated and as such gives the child particular opportunity to explore the third dimension. There are no technical difficulties which should prevent every child having the opportunity to work through the developmental stages of this material, and of course we have a myriad of examples of quite simple and extraordinarily complex clay creations to draw on – from chimney pots to Chinese tomb figures.

The Qin Terracotta Army - China

Since clay is a plastic material in its raw state, it lends itself to the interpretation of certain images and ideas but not to others. For that reason children need to develop skills with rigid materials which allow them to explore strengths and tensions in other structures. Once again there needs to be a considerable opportunity to explore and take risks, testing some materials to breaking point in order to understand their characteristics. Equally however, the precise focus on how one rigid material behaves in contrast to another allows the child to develop a 'knowing through handling', that in the long term creates the possibility of designing and making something with equal consideration to both its aesthetic appeal and function.

Once again we should remember that with all three-dimensional processes, there is an equal need for the child to explore new ideas, imagine and invent. Three-dimensional materials often lend themselves to particular aspects of creativity and for some children, provide the very best way for them to interpret their particular kind of thinking.

There are fundamental characteristics which are common to both music and dance. Certainly they are an equally important part of our central group of interpretive skills, and yet on the one hand they are so different and at the same time so complementary to each other.

When we consider them as we have been considering the different aspects of the visual arts, they too can be broken down in exactly the same way. They are dependent on the same principles and disciplines and they are the medium through which many children find appropriate expression for their ideas. Musicians can and do respond to stimuli and experiences but whereas with the visual arts the creative is in the origination, in music creativity lies both in the origination and interpretation. The performing arts can emulate experience, mirror it, exaggerate, distort it or ridicule it – frequently it is as if they hold up a mirror to life itself and we as teachers want all children to feel those experiences and have the opportunity to interpret them at their own level.

The children I referred
to earlier marching in
the playground were coming
to terms with the first rudimentary
stages of both music and dance – the initial patterns and rhythms
which are so fundamental to our lives and without which even
language would be almost unintelligible, but there was little or no
room in that exercise for creative interpretation.

The first steps on the floor for the dancer are not dissimilar to
the first finger placings for the recorder player. The search is for
developmental progression being in control of self and/or the
instrument in order to be able to interpret or extemporise. This of
course is dependent on the mastery of the medium, the knowing
of self and a desire to communicate feelings, emotions and ideas
that have arisen as a direct result of the impact that the day has
had on our lives.

For most children the earliest stages of Music and Dance are a search for rhythms and patterns, to experiment with these and find sequences in sound or music. The later stages of inventing either sounds or movements oneself are generally built on this early vocabulary.

It goes without saying that even with modern technology the musician and the dancer leave us with a different kind of product to the potter or the painter – their creation is in the moment and the best filming in the world can never give the audience an equal experience to being in the presence of the living performance. Nor can the performer 'feel' the audience through film. I have described earlier the importance of actual experience for children – as they raise their creative expectations, so they raise their creative potential and there are unique experiences in store for children who take part in combined musical or dance performances interpreting the work of great choreographers and musicians and writers.

The importance of live performances in music, dance and drama cannot be over stated, just as the value of the role model of a practising artist in school, working alongside children cannot be measured. All elements come together from their simplest beginnings to enable children to search beyond the norms of their basic learning requirements to reach out to creative possibilities beyond all our dreams.

Whilst I have identified these particular skills as central to my experiences of some disciplines which make creativity possible for children, the list is not definitive. I have indicated where I believe is the best place to start and, since there is so little time in which to cover properly what is fundamental and important, we don't need to pad out the time in the classroom with activities under the name of creativity which could just as easily be done at home, in the street, in fact anywhere except in school.

To use a well-worn cliché "We need to do less, better" and in order to accomplish this model we need to focus all our resources to provide the very best opportunity for children to have the most rigorous and stimulating experiences. The interpretation of experience through creativity will stay with them for the rest of their lives.

It is through our creativity that we come to know and understand the world in which we live. So, the whole of our lives should be seen as one long exciting opportunity for discovery and interpretation.

## Ackowledgements

In conclusion can I offer a generous thankyou to all those teachers and their children who have helped us to finally bring this book together. Without their help none of this would have been possible.

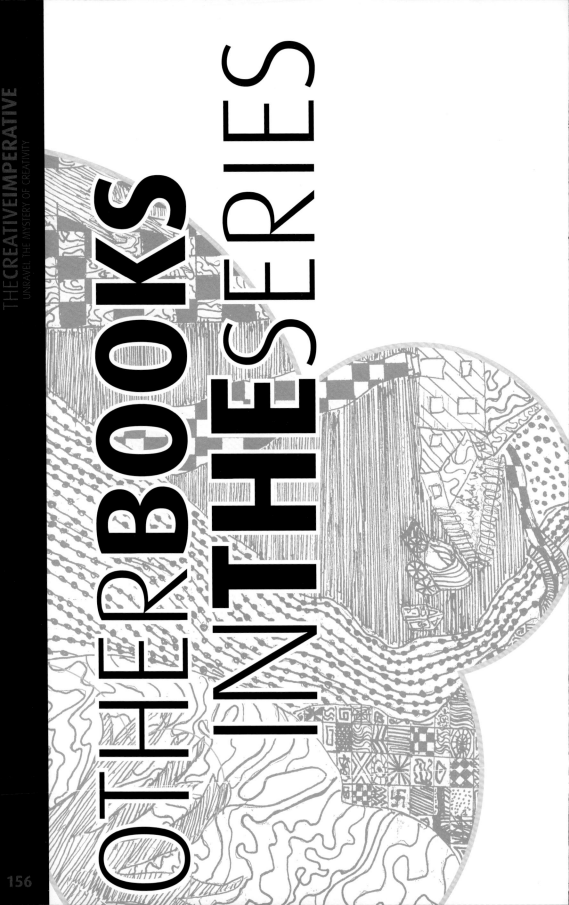

OTHER BOOKS IN THE SERIES

Primary First are specialists in Creativity in the Primary Curriculum. Through our links with NAPE (National Association for Primary Education) and the Royal Shakespeare Company we are publishing some of the most innovative writing on Creativity and all it entails within Primary Education. To order further books in the series from Primary First please call 01543 261925 or order online at www.primaryfirst.com

**Drawing with Children** by Roger Cole                                  £8.50

**Painting with Children** by Roger Cole                                 £8.50

**Classroom Presentation & Display** by Roger Cole          £8.50

**Classroom Organisation & Management** by Roger Cole     £8.50

**Images of Childhood**  by Roger Cole                               £8.50

**Learning about Learning** by Roger Cole                         £8.50

## Coming Soon

**Children are Special by Jo Storrs £30.00 including CD Rom**

**All About Me – because every child matters**

More than a book, 'All About Me' is a foundation for learning. Bright and optimistic, this is a personalised log book of individual development, designed to engage children in the process of recording their own steps forward and to take pride in their actions. Starting at nursery entry, the two books cover Key Stages 1 and 2 and are crammed full of ideas inviting youngsters to record their successes.

The result of detailed consultations with head teachers, educational specialists and government advisers, these books work best with the input of teachers and family members, and encourage children and parents to aim for positive goals and establish values for life.

If you would like to involve your school, or if you are interested in further information, call us on 01543 257257 or visit our website for details www.primaryfirst.com